Art of CHINA, KOREA, AND JAPAN

Art of CHINA,

KOREA, AND JAPAN

PETER C. SWANN

FREDERICK A. PRAEGER, Publishers
NEW YORK • WASHINGTON

BOOKS THAT MATTER

Published in the United States of America in 1963
by Frederick A. Praeger, Inc., Publishers
111 Fourth Avenue, New York 3, N.Y.
Third printing, 1965

Library of Congress Catalog Card Number: 63-18836

Printed in Italy by Amilcare Pizzi - Milan

Contents

Foreword

This book cannot pretend to be more than a very general introduction to a vast subject — an ABC so to speak of three great civilizations of east Asia. It attempts to outline nearly 3,500 years of history and the arts produced by a huge area of the world — an area which now supports well over 700 million people. It is obviously impossible to do more than present the main lines of the developments of these cultures and their arts. In fixing our gaze on the wood we shall inevitably miss a number of individual trees. If the book achieves the aim of every good introduction to a subject it will encourage some readers to look more closely and more deeply through the wealth of material now available in books and museums.

China, Japan and Korea have much in common for they have long been dominated by the cultural power of China. The relative isolation of this huge area from the rest of Asia and the West has contributed greatly to its individuality and its cohesion. It has also set up the kind of tensions which inevitably arise in such a closely knit group. These countries are in a sense a family like the Scandinavians but writ very much larger and with greater differences.

China has been the fountain head of all Far Eastern cultures, and over the centuries Chinese armies have carried its influence over much of the East. Only Japan, protected by a relatively narrow strip of sea, much like the English Channel, and by the vigour of its fighting men, has been able to resist China's armies at all periods. However, this did not prevent her being enthralled by Chinese achievements. With the rise and fall of Chinese power so the cultural impulses to Japan waxed and waned. But Japan was always conscious of her great neighbour's presence, eagerly awaited her manifold inventions and was grateful to receive them. Korea felt the presence of China and of her fiercer neighbours to the north with greater discomfort. She has always been too near, too accessible. No geographical barriers protect Korea from her great continental neighbours. Her culture is thus much closer to that of China than Japan. Much of her literature and some of her art could be interpreted as provincial variations on the main theme. But strangely enough even when following a Chinese pattern, and one thinks particularly of ceramics, Korean products in the Chinese style are more distinctive even than the Japanese. They have their own soft calm.

Korea was the bridge by which cultural innovations passed from China to Japan. At the same time it was also geographically situated to receive influences from the north since her northern frontier was not so well defended as was the Chinese.

Her people are ebullient and gay. Her painting is rich in genre studies, and landscape painting is often powerfully interpreted in a manner which sometimes comes close to eccentricity. Her art has an unpretentious unique flavour which is most difficult to express in words. Of all the Far Eastern nations, we know the least of Korea. The Japanese, during their occupations of that country, discouraged Western interest and, since independence, the Korean scholars themselves have hardly had the time or resources to propagate their achievements. Few private collections exist. Only one great exhibition has been held in the West, and that quite recently. However, the Japanese fortunately were excellent archaeologists and much of our knowledge is due to their diligence and splendid publications.

As Evelyn McCune has pointed out in the only modern history of all Korean arts in a Western language, the Koreans could not afford rich materials and were obliged 'to rely upon beauty of line and shape rather than upon costly materials... It was as if acknowledging inability to compete with the Chinese in magnificence, they made a virtue of necessity and proudly created lovely things out of simple materials by means of techniques of which they were masters. They arrived at strength of expression rather than brilliance and often achieved it with marked success'. The case for Korean art could not be put better.

The manner in which Japan has taken over so many aspects of Chinese civilization has led detractors to accuse her of imitation — just as they did when Japan took over Western forms and methods from the second half of the nineteenth century onwards. However, the Japanese are not just empty imitators. They have created much that is unique and individual within the broad framework of an Eastern approach to art. They are quick to seize an idea and to develop it, refine it, and exploit it in a way which the prodigal Chinese have never troubled to do. The Japanese colour print is an outstanding example of their gifts for the adaptation and development of a theme. In other words, while it is true that much of Japanese art follows styles initiated in China it is also true that very often the Japanese personality makes itself felt in developing them.

The Japanese, as a people, are very different from the Chinese. As far as one can talk of national characteristics, they are less ebullient and extrovert than the Chinese. A sense of humour seldom appears in their daily life whereas, oddly enough, their art shows a lively wit. The reverse is true of the Chinese who are a witty gay people in life but are not generally so in their art. The Chinese are convinced of the superiority of their culture and look inwards. The Japanese are equally convinced of the superiority of their culture, their divine origin etc., but they look outward and accept other people's inventions without being deeply changed by them.

The Japanese have a very materialistic streak and the power which their merchant class gained from about 1600 onwards helped them to adapt themselves with great speed and success to a Western mercantile way of life. The Chinese have always looked down on the merchant trading classes, and their influence on the arts, though present, was less wide-spread. The Chinese scorned the military classes as the lowest stratum of society; the Japanese almost worshipped their fighting men. Even Buddhism, the most pacifistic of all religions was in its Zen form adapted to serve the fighting man.

The deep consciousness of historical continuity which the Japanese enjoy has not made them unmindful of the need for change as it

8

did the Chinese. Rather it gave them an anchor in a constantly changing world. Thus in art the Japanese preserved much which disappeared in China and they have served the historian of Eastern arts well by doing so. For some of the finest examples of Chinese and Korean Buddhist art we must look to Japan, which has never persecuted the Buddhist faith and destroyed its monuments. The Japanese gift for assimilation and empiricism has enabled religious ways of thought as different as Confucianism, Buddhism and Shintoism to live in harmony.

Above all, the Japanese have their own very individual sense of design and colour which is completely different from those of China and Korea. Their designs in painting, colour prints, metal-work, ceramics, embroidery and lacquer are their own — and what a torrent of originality they provide. In these, reticence and outer calm are shattered and burst into gay, almost boundless unrestraint.

Thus to a degree the Japanese, given a basic idea, can be more inventive than the Chinese. Their craftsmen are unsurpassed and for them individuality counts far more than for the Chinese. A craftsman was an artist whom society respected and recompensed and his patrons expected the new and original from him at all times. For the Chinese the crafts are a corporate expression of anonymous workers. In this respect the Japanese practice more closely approaches that of the West. A study of Japanese ceramics from 1600 onwards will convince the student of the unfailing ingenuity, daring and invention of the humblest craftsman.

In a general introduction one can dwell on similarities or differences — we shall try to do both. But in the long run it is the objects themselves which speak. Occasionally one finds something, say a small painting or even a piece of porcelain which could have been made in any of the three countries. Finally the ' expert ' will be forced to say ' I feel it is Japanese ', or ' It has a Korean feel to me '. Unsatisfactory as this may sound, one can develop a sixth sense which comes after long familiarity. A book such as this cannot pretend to teach the reader such discrimination, but it may start him on the long and interesting road towards it.

The journey begins in China ...

1 Vessels of the north-west Chinese Yang-shao culture (third and second millenia BC) of red earthenware finished on a slow wheel. Since buried with the dead, the designs painted on them, eminently suitable for pottery decoration, may also have had a symbolic content of which, alas, we know almost nothing. Geometric motifs enhance their shapes with great calligraphic power. (pp. 11-12)

CHAPTER ONE

The Beginnings

The key to an understanding of almost all the art and culture of east Asia lies in China. Both Korea and then later Japan were to fall under the irresistible influence of their great neighbour who was a thousand years and more ahead of them in the founding of its civilization. Neither Korea nor Japan came into the Chinese orbit until about two thousand years ago and by this time China was reaching the end of a long and distinguished Bronze Age, preceded by a remarkable Stone Age. It is these two periods, singularly isolated from Japanese and Korean history, which must form a long prolegomena to the art of this wide area.

Art as we know it first appeared in the Far East in the middle of the third millenium BC in the late Stone Age. Our knowledge of this period is very inadequate but excavations during the last forty years and particularly in the last ten have enabled us to gain a clear idea of the beginnings. The various cultures which emerged — mostly in the heartland of China (the basin of the Yellow River and its vicinity) — are distinguished by their pottery types. Archaeologists distinguish in this area three main types which developed over a period lasting down to and merging into the period of Shang culture, the first historic period (1523-1028 BC). These three types overlap and often merge. The first type is a splendid red earthenware from the upper Yellow River area (mainly Shensi and Kansu) and characterizes what is known as the Yang-shao culture (*plate* 1). Fashioned by hand, sometimes finished on a slow wheel, the shapes of the vessels are bold and often have painted designs of considerable variety. The meaning

11

2 A Chinese neolithic pottery stand of the Lung-
shan, Shantung, culture with
thin body and black burn-
nished surface. This is a
product of the so-called
'black pottery' culture, contemporary with the slightly
earlier in origin 'red pottery'
culture (plate 1) but of a
technical standard of control
and experimentation far in
advance of it.

of these designs remains obscure to us but many are probably in
origin connected with fertility cults. The Yang-shao potters can be
said to have produced the finest Neolithic pottery of any Stone Age
civilization yet discovered and their skill presages the superiority
of Chinese ceramics in successive centuries. The second culture of the
period comes from the lower Yellow River area and the north-east
coast (mainly Hopei and Shantung) and its characteristic ware is
black or dark brown with burnished surface (*plate 2*). The body of
this type of vessel is often very thin, as little as one eighth of an inch
in thickness, and it was turned on a fast wheel. This culture is known
as Lung-shan from its type site in Shantung. A third culture is known
as Hsiao-t'un from a site on the Yellow River near An-yang which
was to become the last capital of the Shang dynasty, the first historic
dynasty. Its typical pottery is a fine-bodied grey ware produced

12

3 A Chinese neolithic urn of the Hsiao-t'un culture with cord-marking. Hsiao-t'un was near An-yang, in Shansi, which was to become the capital of the Shang dynasty, where production of the great bronzes reached its peak. Hsiaot'un is younger than the Yang-shao and Lungshan cultures.

by the comparatively primitive method of holding a pad inside the vessel and beating the outside with another pad covered with cord or matting which left a pattern on the surface (*plate* 3). On sites where these three cultures are found mixed together the Yang-shao appears to be the oldest and the Hsiao-t'un the youngest.

The above three Neolithic cultures are all found most densely concentrated in the central area of China. In the south-east occurs another type of Neolithic ware which is light grey or brown. Many pieces have geometric impressions on the outside which suggest basket work. In terms of general cultural development, this part of the country was not so advanced as the Yellow River area and the Neolithic culture found there may not date much farther back than the second millennium BC. In places it lasted down into Han times (2nd century BC to 2nd century AD).

The Shang people who created the first dynasty of which we have any material evidence sprang from the Neolithic people who created the Hsiao-t'un culture. Scholars date this dynasty either from 1751 to 1111 BC or from 1523 to 1028 BC. Neither date has been conclusively proved. The earliest discovered capital of the Shang people was at the newly found site of Chêng-chou (serving as capital until 1384 BC according to the earlier dates). It was here that the Shang Chinese discovered (probably independently) the use of bronze. In this material they were to cast some of the finest bronzes the world has known. The Shang people were also skilled bone and jade workers (*plate 5*) and made some marble sculptures. These, however, are somewhat clumsy in comparison with the bronzes. Noblemen enjoyed sizeable homes and palaces and buried their dead in magnificent underground

4 Early Chinese ritual bronze *chüeh*, tripod shaped wine goblet of the pre-An-yang period, found at Chêng-chou, Honan, the capital of the Shang dynasty until 1384 BC. Note the single band of decoration around its waist, with a monster mask, already highly stylized. This is the type of decor which in its fully developed form often entirely fills the surfaces of the An-yang bronzes.

5 Chinese ceremonial bone handle carved with design found mainly on bronzes of this period, twelfth-eleventh century BC.

6 Large Chinese musical stone with incised decoration of a stylized tiger, from the Shang dynasty Great Tomb at Wu-kuan-ts'un, An-yang (plate 7). It was probably suspended from the hole drilled in it in a frame with other such stones and struck to produce ceremonial music. It can be seen in position as buried in the Great Tomb at the bottom left of plate 7.

7 The Chinese Shang dynasty Great Tomb at Wu-kuan-ts'un, An-yang, probably of a nobleman or member of the Shang royal family, with skeletons of sacrificial victims, and, on the left of the pit, the musical stone of plate 6.

burial chambers. Sometimes on these occasions human victims were immolated, in very large numbers for the most exalted dead. They had a flexible and advanced system of writing and practised scapulamancy. This is a type of divination by which they asked their oracle for answers to important questions. They inscribed the questions on bone or tortoise-shell, applied fire and, according to the cracks which appeared, divined the answers. These bones, discovered in their thousands, have provided much important historical and philological material for the characters incised on them are the earliest example of the Chinese script to survive. The typical Shang everyday ware was grey but they also made glazed stoneware and a very fine white ware

8 Two fragments of Chinese scapula bones inscribed for divination by the oracle. The earliest known form of Chinese writing. Shang dynasty.

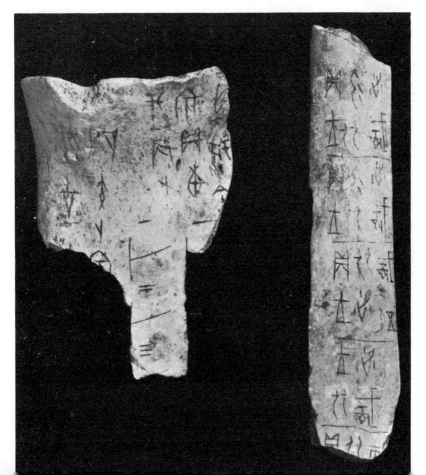

9 Large Chinese Shang dynasty vase from Hsiao-t'un of fine white clay
baked almost to stoneware hardness and remarkably close to the porcelain
not discovered until 2000 years later. The squared spirals, the monster
mask handles and shoulder decoration belong more naturally to bronzes.

(*plate* 9). The ceramic technique was basically that of ring building
but later potters sometimes used a wheel for finishing. These rare
fine white wares have a decoration which is based on that of the
bronzes. Strangely enough, the useful technique of glazing pottery
was subsequently little practised and then abandoned for about
seven hundred years.

10 Shang dynasty bronze ritual wine vessel (*tsun*) in the shape of two rams.
The somewhat crude techniques of Chêng-chou (plate 4) by now perfected.

Without doubt the artistic glory of this age was its bronze work – the finest which any Bronze Age civilization has produced. Eating and cooking vessels, tools, weapons, horse and chariot fittings as well as personal ornaments have been discovered in hundreds in the Shang tombs. And these have occurred in well over one hundred sites over a wide area of central China, stretching from the western borderlands of Kansu to the coast on the east, from just south of Peking almost to the Yangtse. Although produced by the relatively crude method of direct casting into clay moulds, they show a technical excellence and a power of decoration which have never been surpassed.

12 Chinese bronze ritual axe-head of the type used for beheading human sacrificial victims at entombments. Shang dynasty, twelfth-eleventh century BC.

11 Chinese ritual bronze vessel, a square *chia* with a bird (?) knob on its lid. The decoration on this vessel is typical of the high Shang dynasty style (cf. plate 14).

The Shang seem to have discovered the use of bronze independently of the West and even at Chêng-chou in their earliest stage, the vessels show a considerable sophistication. The earliest models for the bronzes may well have been in perishable material such as wood or bone but none of these have survived. At the site of the last Shang capital at An-yang, where their civilization reached its highest level, their art is found in a very highly developed stage. It was only recently, when archaeologists found the previous capital at Chêng-chou, that the more primitive background to the splendours of the An-yang bronzes was revealed (*plate* 4).

13 Early Chou dynasty bronze ritual wine container (*yu*). An extreme, end example of the Shang style with protruding relief, and remarkably realistic monsters at the ends of the handle.

The decoration of these bronzes, basically two-dimensional and linear, is made up of fanciful animal forms including birds and fish, basket patterns and geometric motifs. Although the range of basic motifs is comparatively small, within it there is a great variety of elaboration. The most characteristic decoration was the mysterious monster mask later called *t'ao-t'ieh*. It is, in fact, two dragons seen in profile which, when closely confronted, form what might be a mask.

14 Diagram of a typical *t'ao t'ieh* monster mask taken from a Shang dynasty bronze ritual food vessel (*ting*), showing the various components (after W. Willetts). (plates 4, 11 and 15).

This mask already occurs at Chêng-chou. In the later An-yang bronzes the main elements are further elaborated and often set against a background of minutely cast spirals. The conclusion of this style is a maze of intricate casting in which bold, almost terrifying features seem to explode from a delicate surface. Although the decoration often completely covers the sides of the vessels, on other vessels it can occur in bands leaving parts of the body undecorated. Differences such as this are probably due to different ateliers. Inlay of semi-precious stones or lacquer was occasionally used to embellish the surface.

22

15 Bronze ritual food container of a type (*fang-i*) confined to the Shang dynasty phase of Chinese bronze art, with over all decoration and high ornate seams (cf plates 11 and 14). Note the bird motifs in the panels on the base.

Short inscriptions on the sides or on the base recorded the ancestor to whom the vessel was dedicated, and the maker, or an important event which it celebrates.

Many of the finest vessels were used in ceremonies of ancestor worship and their awesomeness leaves no doubt that they were intended to be objects of the highest religious importance and power, 'arresting symbols of the magical rite of sacrifice' as Watson calls the culminating products of late Shang.

In 1208 BC (according to other chronologies, in 1111) another state, the Chou, overwhelmed the Shang. The Chou were obviously kindred people who had gathered strength by their defence of the frontiers against more barbarous people beyond them, while the Shang, more secure in the centre, had grown enfeebled. The Chou people must have admired and envied the Shang, for when they assumed the power in central China they adopted Shang culture and the art that it had produced. In China strong but uncultured people have often overrun cultured but feeble regimes in the centre and taken over the civilization of the people they conquered.

The Chou period lasted *de jure* for over seven hundred years but they ruled in fact only until about 771 BC. After that the expanding states of China grew increasingly independent. Warfare between them was at first a chivalrous affair but in the Warring States period (480-221 BC) it became increasingly ruthless and annihilation was the penalty of defeat. This was the period of the Hundred Schools of Philosophy of which Confucius founded only one – and for the time an unsuccessful one at that. In a period of political disintegration he appealed for a return to the largely imaginary standards of an ideal antiquity of early Chou.

In 221 BC the least conservative, best organised and most savage of the many states, that of Ch'in, defeated its last rival and united China for the first time. This state, despite the pious hopes of its founders, lasted only a comparatively short time – less than twenty years (221-206) – but it paved the way for the succeeding four hundred years of the Han period in which the first great Chinese Empire was created. The beginning of this period coincides with China's emergence from its Bronze Age and into its modern period. For the first time,

16 Chinese bronze bell of the fifth-fourth century BC (the Warring States period). The interlocking snake motif is sometimes known as the mark of the Huan style from the river valley in which it was first found, although examples of this style and period have been found all over north central China.

as we shall see in the next chapter, the organised might of a united China reached out beyond the confines of China to embrace Korea.

It is impossible to distinguish many of the bronzes produced in the early Chou from those of late Shang. Shang craftsmen survived and Shang taste obviously persisted. After about a century the Chou style began to assert itself. Some of the characteristic Shang shapes disappeared altogether. A marked tendency towards a decorative and less

17 Chinese ritual bronze food vessel (*kuei*) of about 1000 BC, with dragon-headed handles, (cf plate 103). The style of this vessel is almost typical of the coming mid-Chou dynasty phase. There is not such profusion of detail and protuberance, the dragons under the rim are snake-like and not as ebullient as in the Shang style. (cf plate 15).

symbolically loaded treatment is evident and the surfaces are smoother, the decoration often flat and not in such high relief. These tendencies were carried further in bronzes produced in the late ninth to early eighth century BC. These are certainly less terrifying objects than those of the Shang.

In 771 BC the Chou kings, under pressure from western areas of China, moved their capital to Lo-yang in central Honan, which, as a result of its more central position they considered safer. From this

18 Chinese bronze chariot fitting in the shape of a bull's head inlaid with gold and silver, of the fifth-fourth century BC. This remarkable example of naturalistic animal representation belongs to the period covering the end of Chou to the Han dynasty, and is a product of Chin-t'sun, Honan, where workshops specialized in ornate inlay, another characteristic of this period.

time onwards they had little effective power and the lords surrounding them only tolerated the Chou House since it was responsible for the main sacrifices and because none of them was yet strong enough individually to take over the undisputed leadership. The bronzes of this period are rarer and more difficult to distinguish, yet, despite the political upheaval, casting techniques rose to the most refined standards. The patterns became broader and designs of interlacing dragons or snakes are frequently found. One of the most characteristic features

19 Chinese ritual bronze wine vessel (*hu*) of the fifth-fourth century BC, with panels showing hunting scenes. The occurence of human figures (perhaps the feathered immortals of Chinese mythology), is rare on early bronzes; it marks a growing tendency to humanize that leads into Han dynasty art. (pp 29-30)

20 Chinese bronze pair of wrestlers or acrobats probably intended for burial and the entertainment of the deceased in after-life, fifth-third centuries BC. A piece unusual in its portrayal of human beings in the round.

is the reappearance of the animal masks, such a feature of late Shang – early Chou bronzes, but here treated more decoratively than in the early bronzes and serving to set off the complicated decorations on the bodies of vessels, decorations which again tend to fill the whole surface.

Towards the end of the Chou years the designs became even more minute, and the shapes smoother and more gentle. Sometimes gold and silver inlays lighten and enrich the surfaces. Local styles can be distinguished. Naturalistic animal forms appear on lids and handles– elements of which probably came from nomadic art. The whole effect is of an art in the process of being adapted from the service of the gods to that of man. Recognisably human figures also appear for the first time – notably figures of northerners. One of the most remarkable groups of figures come from Ch'ang-sha in Hunan, and one in particular made of lacquered wood with painted designs (*plate* 21). They date from the third century BC and are early examples of tomb figures, so popular in the Han and T'ang dynasties to come.

The other material which characterises the first 1500 years of Chinese art is jade. Used for tools and decorative beads in Neolithic times, under the Shang and Chou it emerged as an art medium in its own right. The word 'jade', probably of Spanish origin, was introduced into Europe in the early eighteenth century to describe newly discovered pre-Columbian objects. Geologists distinguish jadeite from nephrite but the ancient Chinese did not. To them both of these hard stones were *yü*, defined in a second century AD dictionary simply and adequately as 'a stone that is beautiful'. This criterion in the main, and that it is hard, smooth and cold, seems to have been the only one which influenced the Shang craftsmen. They mastered the technique of shaping and drilling this extremely hard stone, and from it fashioned handles, ceremonial blades, discs, tubes, pendants, and arrow heads. Among the most interesting of the early jade objects are the many figures of animals. In silhouette they show the same vitality as those on the bronzes would lead one to expect. Decoration on early jades is produced by raised or incised lines. Pendants were generally made from a flat piece of jade but a few sculptures in the round have also survived. Technically many of the jades show the finest craftsmanship. The perforations which some have are often of the most extraordinary accuracy considering the intractability of the material.

However, compared with what the Chou centuries produced, the Shang jade objects are little more than primitive. Chou craftsmen carved the most complicated objects – still largely ceremonial and decorative – achieving a standard of workmanship equal to that of subsequent centuries, even the eighteenth century AD when the art reached a new standard of excellence (see p. 225)

It is easy for us to appreciate the visual beauty of jade and its delight to the touch but to the early Chinese it was much more. It may well have been to them the essence of power or virtue. They obviously

21 Human figure in wood with painted lacquer decoration, of the third century BC, from Ch'ang-sha in the Yangtze valley, Hunan. This product of a south Chinese culture is quite distinct from that of north China. The southern culture, whose stronghold was the virtually independent state of Ch'u in Chou times and whose mythology as for instance in the Ch'u Tz'u (Song of Ch'u), was richer and more colourful than that of the north, was to be absorbed by the Han as their control spread over the whole of China.

22 A Chinese Shang dynasty jade pendant in the form of a stag, probably intended as dress decoration for burial with dead.   A fine example
of early naturalism, showing an art of silhouette and organic simplification
at which the Chinese have always excelled.

took great pains to obtain the material, probably from central Asia or Siberia, through trade with the nomad peoples who were by tradition their enemies. It was used in religious and secular ceremonies of all kinds both for the living and the dead – a custom which survived down to the last century. All the virtues which the West sees in pearls and diamonds, the Chinese see in jade, and the Confucian scholar moralising in the second century AD adds to the definition of jade as simply 'A stone that is beautiful' the following: 'It has five virtues; there is warmth in its lustre and brilliancy, this is the manner of kindness; its soft interior may be viewed from outside revealing (the goodness) within, this is the manner of rectitude; its note is tranquil and high and carries far and wide, this is the way of wisdom; it may be broken but cannot be twisted, this is the manner of bravery; its sharp edges are not intended for violence, this is the way of purity'. These surely summarise attitudes of many centuries of appreciation.

What was the legacy of this two to three thousand year formative period? First, from the artistic point of view, the Chinese discovered and exploited many of the materials and techniques in which their genius was later to find abundant expression. Art became respected as a servant of the divine and from this grew an appreciation of the need for fine craftsmanship. A repertoire of shapes, some of which survive to the present day, was created.

From the philosophical point of view, the two basic Chinese attitudes of thought, manifested as Confucianism and Taoism, were first defined. The one is rational, objective and tradition loving, the other irrational, mystical and non-conformist. The interplay of these two contradictory ways of thought has created much of Chinese and therefore much of east Asian art.

23 Rubbing from a stone relief in a Chinese tomb of the Han dynasty depicting
the legend of Hou Yi, the divine archer, shooting down nine of the ten suns in
the form of birds . These had risen all at the same time from the tree of the eastern horizon and were scorching the earth. (p. 51)

CHAPTER TWO

The first Chinese Empire
Beginnings of Korean and Japanese cultures

With the creation of the Han Empire, China for the first time became a world power. In the wake of her armies Chinese culture began to reach out beyond her natural frontiers. The founder of the Ch'in state had put an end to the feudal period by ruthlessly uniting the country and, hated though he was, he created the basic concept of a united China. To this fundamental idea the Chinese subsequently held, throughout the vicissitudes of their national history. The long Han dynasty (206 BC - AD 221) reaped the benefit of the Ch'in Emperor's work.

Its régime marked the final breakdown of the traditional ways of life idealised by the Chou. Its founder was a commoner. Hitherto in China the principle of the 'Mandate of Heaven', the authority by which a king ruled, had applied only to the nobility. Henceforth this fundamental political theory could apply equally to a man who did not belong to the traditional ruling class. Of equal importance, it could also apply to a foreigner. Over the following two thousand years many were to appeal to it. The Japanese, with their belief in the divinity of their royal house, never adopted this theory. There the struggle for power went on behind the façade of an inviolable imperial authority and even then it was not until 1615 that a man of humble origins reached supreme authority in the land.

The energy of the Chinese race, hitherto spent in almost continuous interstate warfare, now exploded north, east and west into lands beyond the proper borders of China. The new rulers personally were attracted by the magic of popular Taoism, a debased derivative of the early philosophers. This offered them such blandishments as the elixir of immortality or communication with the dead. But at the same time they were shrewd enough to appreciate that this kind of sorcery, even though backed by a primitive church organisation, was not an instrument by which they could rule a huge country. The Ch'in state had ruled China by applying a harsh legalist code, but once the Han dynasty was firmly established this was found inadequate for times of peace and was discredited. The only available dogma with an educated following capable of administering China was Confucianism – the scholarly ethic which was to inspire (and restrict) its followers for the next two thousand years. The despotism of Ch'in and also of early Han enabled Confucius to triumph more than three centuries after his death! Thus began a tradition of government by cultured literary men which was to have a lasting influence on all the arts. Membership of the administrative élite was no longer a birthright. One became an official by examination, always theoretically, and often practically, open to high and low-born alike. So interest in scholarship (notably Confucian) and the arts became very broadly based. A civil servant and man of culture was expected to have an interest in the arts in the broadest sense; he might be a painter, a critic, a poet, a collector or an historian. One can understand how this Chinese ideal appealed to European gentlemen of the seventeenth-eighteenth centuries!

The Han period was one of new confidence and adventure. The world as the Chinese knew it expanded in all directions. Rumours of Indian Buddhism, later to influence the whole of the Chinese culture, first reached China. In the far west of Asia another great empire, that of Rome, flourished and provided a distant market for Chinese silks, a market which the Chinese only suspected and which they supplied through countless middlemen across Central Asia. Adventurous raids beyond the static fortifications of the Great Wall neutralised the traditional enemies of China, the ever-watchful and envious nomads of the northern plains. Chinese diplomats and armies faced the unknown perils of Central Asia in their search both for allies against the elusive nomads and for the superior breeds of horses which would give the Han troops a military advantage over them. A proud spirit filled the land and the Chinese, whatever the odds they were called on to face, whatever losses their armies suffered, refused even to contemplate defeat.

Without any doubt a completely new spirit infused Han art. The lingering mystery of the early Bronze Age had now disappeared completely and an art *of* man and his natural world *for* man and his own society took its place. Until the Han, Chinese artistic thought seems to have been turned in upon itself. Now it looked outward. Fashion began to play its part and for the first time we can share the emotions of this distant civilization.

24 Fragment of Chinese Han dynasty woven silk, found in the dry areas of northwest China by Sir Aurel Stein. Marks of silk wrapping on buried Shang dynasty bronzes are evidence of the already long tradition of the silk industry in China even by Han times.

25 The decorated backs of two late Chou-Han dynasty Chinese bronze mirrors. The T pattern on the lower one is peculiar to the mirrors but its background of comma-curl and the zigzag scroll and rudimentary bird motifs of the upper are common on Han silk and lacquer.

Its art became universal. Bronze ritual vessels continued to be made but in small numbers and in a very restricted range of forms. The Ch'in conquest had made man discontinue and even forget the rituals for which the early bronzes had been made. The new bronzes were often plain vases similar in shape to those of pottery with rings held by simplified animal masks. They also used bronze for coins, drums and weapons but the craftsmen seem to have reserved their best technique for bronze mirrors whose backs carry a wide range of decorations. They had first been made in the late Chou period but the main part of their development was under the Han. Some have complicated and very imaginative designs based on animal motifs but the most typical show human figures seated or riding in chariots in a new naturalistic manner. Some have mythical figures taken from the wide range of Han superstitious beliefs. Even so the approach of Chinese artists is here more relaxed than in earlier centuries.

26 Back of a Chinese bronze mirror with scenes of a hunt and two of mythical creatures divided by geometric designs based on an elaborate scroll formation inlaid in gold and silver. Made in Chin-ts'un, Honan famous for its inlay work of this period, late Chou-Han dynasty.

Ceramics show the changed attitude to art most immediately. With peace came wealth and with the downfall of the old noble classes, wealth and civil position became the qualification for those privileges formerly belonging to them, such as exalted burial. But bronze was in short supply, difficult to work and expensive. Thus in an expanding society pottery vessels replaced those of bronze for the tomb. Many of them were glazed, a technique dating from before Han times but mastered for the first time on a large scale by Han potters.

The most common type of Han pottery is of red or grey earthenware and carries a dark green (less often a brown or yellow) glaze which acquires a lively iridescence after burial just as bronze gains an attractive patina. The shapes were sturdy and the intricacies of bronze design were smoothed away. The Chinese gift for concentration and refinement of form in ceramics was developed in this period. Only the occasional animal mask harks back to early times. The large number of Han tombs uncovered throughout the whole of China have yielded not only simple pots but also a whole new range of objects in this ware. It includes models of buildings ranging from a simple outside closet to a towering pleasure tower with many storeys complete with inhabitants (*plate* 28). Other objects give a vivid insight into Chinese life of the times – a cooking stove complete with imple-

27 Han dynasty Chinese green-glazed earthenware jar with monster mask and ring-handle design, exactly reproducing that on the bronze vessel of which this is a reproduction — bronze being too costly a material for the increasing demand for such vessels in the Han dynasty. Shapes that belonged intrinsically to ceramic art began to appear only later.

28 Chinese Han dynasty tomb model of a towered pleasure pavilion complete with inhabitants, in pale green glazed earthenware. Such models provide valuable evidence of wooden architectural styles long since vanished. The style of such towers as this, mentioned in the Classics as belonging to Dukes along with hunting parks and lakes is one possible prototype for pagodas.

ments, a granary, a pig sty or chicken run, in fact models of all the impedimenta of daily life reproduced in miniature to serve the dead in the next world. These objects were made with a careful observation which is part of that search for naturalism which guided the endeavours of Chinese potters in this field for many centuries to come. At the same time they show a humour which is new in Chinese art. A dark grey unglazed earthenware was also made. The attraction of

29 Chinese Han dynasty green glazed earthenware model of a cooking stove complete with implements and food, to serve the dead in the next world.

both wares is often the designs painted on them in black, white, red and green unfired pigments. Both types sometimes have impressed or painted landscape scenes in which intrepid horsemen hunt deer through the hills. Landscape is also found modelled on the conical lids of 'hill jars' which are supposed to represent the Taoist paradise or 'Island of the Blessed' whose denizens enjoy immortality and eternal youth.

30 Chinese Han dynasty earthenware tomb models of players at some kind of board game. The green glaze on this and so much Han pottery is the most common of the limited range at this period, although brown and yellow are also found. A fine iridescence of the glaze was acquired through burial.

31 Chinese Han dynasty Yüeh ware (see plates 32,33) tomb models in the form of two small dishes, one a sheep in a pen, the other a pig in a sty.

Far more important in the history of ceramics than these pottery types, however, was a highly fired stoneware with brown or olive green glaze which was first produced early in this period or even slightly before. This so-called Yüeh ware was first produced at the Tê-ch'ing and Nine Rocks kilns in Chekiang. Its superior quality rapidly won high appreciation and early connoisseurs invested it with almost magical powers. Its importance lies in the fact that it was the first of a long line of celadon wares which, as a Japanese expert has said, form the backbone of Chinese ceramics. The Chinese continued to make these Yüeh wares down to the tenth century and through them one can trace the developments of Chinese ceramics up to the invention of pure porcelain.

The Han centuries also saw the beginning of large sculpture in the round – though its scarcity suggests that the Chinese were not at first attracted greatly to the medium. At the tomb in Shensi of General Ho Ch'ü-ping who died in 177 BC are some large horses roughly fashioned from boulders (*plate* 34). They are crude in execution but some of them have a surging vitality which matches their hugeness.

Winged chimeras were also a favourite theme in late Han sculpture and one can trace the increasing refinement of treatment and mastery of conception in the round in these mythical beasts throughout the following four centuries. However it was not until the introduction of Buddhism that China produced sculpture on a scale to match its other artistic creativity. Buddhism too was to turn the attention of sculptors predominantly to the human form.

It is true that naturalistic figures of animals and even humans appeared in the centuries before the Han period – particularly in bronze – but they were comparatively few. From this time onwards they began to form an increasing element in Chinese art. Part of the new interest was the result of nomad influences in the Central Kingdom.

One of the most serious northern threats came from the Hsiung-nu who formed a powerful tribal union from the third century BC onwards. They had close contacts with the Chinese and there seems to have been an easy give and take of population between them. The nomads welcomed Chinese emigrants as scribes, administrators, officials and even farmers. Their leaders always looked to China as a source of quick plunder, particularly when severe winters created an acute winter food shortage. Their most ambitious ruler came into

32, 33 Two examples of the earliest known Chinese Yüeh ware, third century BC. From this highly fired brown glaze ware the Chinese developed the superb celadon porcelains of a thousand years later (see plate 125). It can be seen how the shapes and decoration of these pots are still very much those of metalwork.

34 Chinese stone horse standing over a fallen barbarian from the tomb of General Ho Ch'ü-ping in Shensi province, died 117 BC. (p. 44)

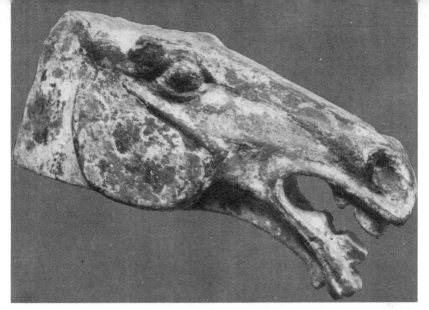

35 Chinese Han dynasty pottery horse's head from a tomb figure. The modelling here is far more accomplished than in the figure opposite, Han sculptors being more experienced in clay than in stone. The type of horse portrayed is west Asian, to obtain which Han armies crossed Central Asia as far as Ferghana, near Samarkand.

conflict with other leaders within the confederation when he asserted that if they were to rule China they must do so from within and this would involve giving up their traditional nomadic way of life. Later nomad invaders of China were very willing to make this basic change; they became Chinese, within a century or so losing their identity.

The early Han rulers tried to pacify the nomads by bribery – by giving them supplies and luxury articles and by sending them Chinese princesses in marriage – but relations between the two peoples were never marked by confidence or ease. As the Han empire became more prosperous and powerful, fewer Chinese went over to the 'barbarians', bribes were less willingly given and the Hsiung-nu were forced to take ever more desperate measures.

Soon the Chinese adopted a more active warlike policy towards the Hsiung-nu. It was partly the needs of trade which forced this idea upon them, since they had to control the profitable routes to the west. Equally they needed to protect themselves. The Great Wall had proved inadequate. Emperor Wu (141-86 BC) was particularly energetic in carrying the war deep into the nomad territory – often with tremendous losses to his armies. The famous expedition of Chang Ch'ien across Central Asia almost to the borders of the Roman Empire was inspired by a desire to find allies against the Hsiung-nu. The conquest of western Kansu, the west China province leading into Central Asia, was also dictated by anti-nomad policy – the need to prevent the northern nomads from making common cause with the Tibetans. The danger from the Hsiung-nu was not ended until the first century BC (even then only temporarily) when the southern half of the tribes came under Chinese control. But other nomad tribes gathering their forces in the north, west and east were ready to take their place – notably the Hsien-pei.

In order to defeat the northern horsemen, the Chinese were forced to become skilled in cavalry warfare. This and the increased contacts of diplomacy brought them into close touch with nomad art which was generally expressed in small objects such as horse-trappings and personal adornments. The art of the nomad peoples who ranged from one end of Asia to the other was dominated by animal themes in which violent combat played a large part. The Chinese seem to have been fascinated by these new and energetic art forms. The animal combat motif began to appear in Chinese art and in particular influenced Chinese bronzes and jades – notably in personal adornments like belt hooks. Finely modelled snarling bears in gilt bronze (*plate* 37) are a notable northern form which the Chinese adopted. Even the dragons of the period acquired a new aggressive air. In all these innovations one senses that fashion is playing a part and that the Chinese were quick to enjoy something new. One can share the excitement which knowledge of an expanding world brought to Chinese artists at every level.

In lacquer objects also, this new sense of swirling movement found expression in the decoration of boxes, plates and cups. Lacquer, like jade, is a characteristic feature of Eastern civilizations and the Chinese seem to have used it as early as the Shang dynasty when occasionally it served to fill in the decoration of bronzes. At the start of the Han dynasty it had just become a major industry. Now its products were used by the wealthy and even prized by the more distant tribes of

36 Bronze trapping from the nomad culture of the
Ordos region beyond the Great Wall, before and
contemporary with the Han dynasty. This animal-
centred art had a strong influence on China.

37 Chinese Han dynasty gilt bronze bear, possibly
a support for a piece of furniture or a large dish; a
result of nomad art influence.

38 Chinese early Han dynasty impressed and painted grey clay tile from Chin-
ts'un, Honan, such as lined the richer tombs. The aggressive hooks and swirls
of this dragon can be seen as abstract motifs on Han mirrors, lacquer and silk
(plates 25, 26, 39).

north and central Asia as something especially valuable. The backgrounds of Han lacquer are generally of a soft dark brown and the designs, based on schematic bird and animal forms, are painted in red with remarkable fantasy. Nothing shows the sophistication of Han upper class society better than its lacquer (*plates* 39, 40).

From painting in lacquer it is only a short stop to painting proper. To this period belong the few earliest fragments of painting which

39 Chinese Han dynasty lacquer bowl painted with bird, dragon and cloud-scroll motifs. Lacquer was a large and flourishing luxury industry at this time especially in the west of China, in Szechwan.

40 Chinese painted lacquer basket from a tomb at Lolang, the capital of the Chinese military colony in Korea. The painting of the gentlemen in conversation is typical of the easy linearity, the naturalistic new interest in human beings, and the effort to solve the problems of spatial organisation in Han representational art.

have survived. The stone slabs of tombs carved in low relief provide ample evidence of the powers of pictorial organisation of Han artists. As has often been pointed out, these designs with their emphasis on movement and outline belong more to painting than to sculpture. Occasionally a real painting has survived; the best known example being a tomb tile in Boston showing spectators at an animal fight. The powers of representation of character are already well developed and the artists are feeling their way towards the representation of depth (*plate* 41).

As well as expanding its control and administration of China proper, Han China became imperialist and its armies established their first colonies in a foreign country. The country nearest to them for this purpose was Korea, and knowledge of what has been found in Korea from this period is essential for understanding Han art.

The mountainous territory of Korea, a land about the size of England, Scotland and Wales, forms a peninsula reaching out from Manchuria towards the islands of Japan – a position of great importance

51

41 Section of a Han dynasty
painted tomb tile in which the
human figures watching an animal
fight are represented in an even
more naturalistic and alive manner
(cf plate 40). Chinese painting has
here developed a sense of reces-
sion and increased movement,
already a very calligraphic art.

42 Detail of a Chinese late Han dynasty tomb wallpainting in Wang Tu, Hupei province, showing an official painted in yellow, blue and red with black outlines. The figure may represent a member of the state courier service attending the funeral. In these paintings, as in so much Chinese art, the draughtsmanship is the most remarkable feature.

for the transmission of mainland cultural movements to those islands. Communications with China have always been easy and while culturally she has gained from this proximity, politically she has frequently suffered. Her role in the arts of the East has been admirably summarised by Gompertz as follows: 'throughout her long history Korea has been deeply influenced by Chinese culture, but it would be a great mistake to assume that Korean art is therefore only a poor imitation of what she received from China. On the contrary... after an initial stage when Chinese models were closely copied, distinctively Korean characteristics invariably appeared and, in the final outcome, Korea made a definite contribution of her own in all the principal fields of art: in architecture, sculpture, painting, and ceramics the Korean artistic expression is quite distinct and unique.'

We know relatively little about the earliest periods in Korea. As far back as the third millennium BC the population of the country was mainly that of the north Asian tribes who lived by hunting and fishing. The language of Korea is allied to the Altaic speaking people of the north rather than to the Chinese group of languages and the early pottery is akin to that of north China and the northern plateau. Over thousands of years the country must have received influxes from the north which brought a northern type of religion based on shamanism, elements of which have survived. As also with the Japanese, a strong animistic strain persisted. In the fourth century BC the expanding Hsiung-nu peoples pushed the Tungusic peoples of Manchuria into Korea, and these emigrants brought with them a knowledge of iron and bronze. From the third century BC Chinese culture and with it a knowledge of agriculture began to influence north-west Korea. The first state was established in 190 BC in the north-west and was known as Choson with its capital at P'yongyang. Thus when the Chinese invaded the country to prevent an alliance between Choson and their enemies the Hsiung-nu, they found a culture which was a mixture of northern and Chinese elements. They destroyed Choson in 10 BC and established four commanderies of which only one, Lo-lang, was still surviving by 75 BC. It flourished as a result of its trading position and only fell in AD 313 to the ever hostile Koreans when northern invasions of China proper interrupted communications.

43 Belt buckle of beaten gold inlaid with turquoise. This, the finest example of Chinese Han dynasty jewellery, was excavated at Lolang, (near the present day P'yongyang, Korea) which was the capital of a Chinese commandery from 108 BC to AD 313. This was the agency of great Chinese influence on the development of Korean and hence early Japanese art.

Some of the most remarkable Han inspired objects come from excavations of this period (*plate* 43).

Surrounding this Chinese outpost three native Korean states grew up - Koguryo in the north, Paekche in the south-west and Silla in the south-east. The beginnings of their native art belong to the next chapters but before passing on to this we must take a brief look at the world of the Japanese islands in this early period.

Our knowledge of the origins of the Japanese people remains unclear. They would appear to be a very complex mixture of south-east Asian and north-east Asian strains with more of the latter than the former. Their comparative isolation, effected by a sea about 150 miles wide separating them from Korea, and the fact that Japan has never been conquered by Chinese armies has always given Japan more cultural distinction than Korea. But what the Chinese could do in Korea by force of arms they did in Japan by the example of their superior civilization. The language, like that of Korea, belongs to the northern Asiatics rather than to China. The extensive researches of Japanese archaeologists enable us to know more about Neolithic Japan than we do about Korea. Early Japanese culture, closely related to that of the north Asiatic mainland lasted from at least the second millennium BC down to the third century AD when contacts with the advanced culture of China swept Japan into its modern period. In doing so Japan almost entirely skipped a Bronze Age.

44 Japanese pottery vessel of the Middle Jōmon period built up in rings by hand and with heavy cord-marked decoration.

45 Japanese Middle Jōmon period clay figurine, small but with monumental quality. This semi-human, semi-feline figure of some spirit comes at a transitional stage in the development of Jōmon figurines after which portrayals of human beings predominate. Perhaps it marks the breakdown of a totemic system.

46 Japanese Late Jōmon clay figurine, dated by some experts as far back as the first millenium BC. A female figure, which appears to have been treasured and fondled as a fertility idol by the ancient Japanese women, perhaps a precursor of the Ainu goddess of the hearth.

The first long part of this early period is called Jōmon, a name taken from the technique of decorating their pottery by impressing the surface with twisted cords. The pots are heavy and clumsy but for an early people show great imagination and an ability to deal with complex decorative schemes. More interesting than the pottery are the clay figurines produced in the later centuries of this era. We do not know what part these strangely moving figures played in the primitive animistic religion of the early Japanese but they were probably fertility symbols of some kind. Though small in size they have an almost monumental power which makes an immediate appeal to Western taste for so-called 'primitive' art.

The Jōmon culture was displaced by that of the Yayoi in about the third to second century BC which brought with it agriculture and knowledge of bronze and iron. Yayoi is also the name of the reddish-brown pottery that was brought in by this new culture. It was probably influenced from the mainland and was much finer and made on

the wheel. From this time onwards the centre of Japanese culture was in the area stretching from north Kyūshū to the Kinki area and embracing Osaka, Kyōto and Kōbe. This culture in its turn received further influences from the mainland and around the third century AD was established what is known as the 'Old Tomb Period' characterised by its custom of burial in huge man-made mounds often surrounded by moats. The objects in these tombs included much fine craftsmanship from China, notably bronze mirrors. Of particular interest, however, were the clay figures which were placed on and around the tombs. The idea of such figures must have originated in China but the Japanese products are quite distinct from anything made there. Human beings, animals, houses, boats etc., give a striking insight into the life, dress and customs of the time. Simply modelled they have a strange and impressive haunted expression. Naïve yet highly eloquent they show the Japanese artistic genius before full and direct contact with China for a time overwhelmed it.

47 Tumulus tomb of the Japanese Emperor Nintoku, AD 139-427, near Osaka, with the key-hole shape surrounded by moats characteristic of the Old Tomb Period. The main burial chamber is under the circular part of the key-hole, the bottom part being a kind of platform, a grand approach to the tomb.

48, 49, 50 Three examples of Japanese Haniwa clay tomb figures of the Old Tomb period — a woman, probably a shaman; a warrior in bamboo slat and leather bound armour; and a monkey. Haniwa figures topped long cylinders which were pressed into the earth around the tomb so that the figures were on the ground lining the approach to the place of burial.

51 Detail from a tomb wall painting at T'ung-kou in Manchuria, fifth-sixth
century AD. Han, Chinese and Central Asian styles are combined in this chase
through a stylized landscape. The figure on horseback, shooting over his shoulder
is the famous Western motif of the 'Parthian horseman'.

CHAPTER THREE

Disunion in China
Buddhism
Japan enters the Chinese orbit

The downfall of the Han dynasty after four centuries of almost un-broken rule left China divided and a prey to the northern peoples. The fall of the Han followed a pattern which was to become familiar in later centuries. The ruling house grew debilitated: the twin evils of eunuch rule and palace intrigue beset politics and undermined the administration. The peasantry became helplessly impoverished or at worst slaves to the large landowners whose estates grew at their expense. The economic life of the country was slowly strangled.

A confused period followed from 221 to 589 AD which saw the country divided into northern and southern areas. In the north various adventurers or foreign kings created kingdoms while in the south remnants of Chinese royal families and adventurers defended them-selves from each other and against the more serious threat from the north. China under the Northern and Southern Dynasties or 'The Six Dynasties' was disunited and in economic distress. Yet this politi-cally debased period was one of deep intellectual and moral reassess-ment. The Chinese began seriously to question the validity of their standards and sought basic reasons for the disappearance of their former glory. They began to realise that they were not the only civilized country in the world nor the centre of a universe which they ruled by unquestioned right of superior culture. The Japanese were not to pass through a similar fire until the late nineteenth cen-tury when the West forced it upon them.

In this sad period, which the Chinese consider their equivalent of our Dark Ages, without doubt the most important factor was the victory of the Buddhist faith. This great religion, originating in India in the sixth and fifth centuries BC, slowly made its way through the oasis kingdoms in the desert of Central Asia at about the time of Christ and first entered China in the first century AD. As Han institutions disintegrated, so Buddhism made progress, and the Chinese began the long process by which they adapted the Indian model to suit their own needs.

To the Buddhists life is full of suffering whose cause is desire. Salvation comes through the eradication of desire and the way to this is through the eight-fold Path – right views, intentions, speech, conduct, livelihood, effort, mindfulness, and concentration. The ultimate goal is a complete extinction in *nirvana* which brings the ending of the chain of successive deaths and rebirths and hence of the suffering they entail. Fundamentally such a consummation made little appeal to the Chinese whose traditions had always been those of ancestor worship. They preferred the Mahayana, or 'Greater Vehicle', concept as opposed to the Hinayana, or 'Lesser Vehicle', which involves the purer concept of death as a void and *nirvana* as final extinction. The Mahayana offered endless stepping stones along the path to *nirvana*. These took the form of paradises inhabited by a whole pantheon of divinities – notably the Bodhisattvas, beings whose series of good lives entitled them to enter *nirvana* but who delayed the final release in order to help suffering humanity. They and the various Buddhas they served were of prime importance in Far Eastern iconography.

The gulf which separates Indian language and thought from those of China is very wide and it was not until the disorders of late Han and after had convinced thinking people of the seeming failure of Chinese ways of thought that the general population was ready to listen to the alien but profound Indian ideas of personality, time, space and salvation. Translation from Sanscrit, the original language of Buddhism, into Chinese posed great problems and reasonable translations of the Indian scriptures only began to appear late in the third century. The Chinese first had to find readily understandable Chinese concepts by which to translate Indian Buddhist ideas. The more abstruse concepts came slowly. Nevertheless, by about AD 300 nearly a thousand works had been translated and numerous Buddhist establishments had spread over the north and south of China. Indian missionaries came to China and Chinese seekers like Fa Hsien made the dangerous journey to study in India (AD 399-413). Great translators like Kumārajīva who arrived in Ch'ang-an in AD 401 established large-scale translating bureaux and their work began to give the Chinese a deeper understanding of the scriptures.

Meanwhile in the north contacts with the various nomad tribes became closer. The Chinese there allied themselves first with one group and then with another, sometimes even providing their fierce neighbours with food and weapons in the vain hope of remaining unmolested. In 311 Loyang, a city of 600,000 people, fell to the northern invaders and was sacked. The traditional enemies of Chinese culture thus firmly occupied the heartland of China. Those Chinese who could escape fled to the south, to the Yangtse regions which in the wake of the Han civilization were only just being brought into the Chinese orbit. There, during a series of short dynasties, they clung to the ancient Han traditions and wistfully dreamed of restoring unity to China. The northern horsemen could not operate successfully in the mountainous terrain and steamy climate of the south, and, after a number of rebuffs, were content to leave it alone. The most successful of these southern dynasties was that of the Liang (502-577 AD) which enjoyed a capable and devout ruler in Emperor Wu who reigned 502-549 AD. But many Chinese were forced to remain in the north, there to work out their own salvation with the 'barbarians' to survive as best they could the periodic slaughters and to make the most of times of appeasement.

Buddhism rapidly gained strength in both north and south. The northerners envied Chinese culture but distrusted Confucianism. Thus they were prepared to accept the alien deity and its foreign monks in preference to anything traditionally Chinese. It seems that the Buddhist monks were first considered as little more than superior magicians and their teachings as another form of neo-Taoism. Subsequently the alien rulers realised that they were the only educated body apart from the Confucians which could help them govern and thus profit from the lands they had won by the sword.

Those Chinese who were lucky enough to ride out the storms in north China lost faith in both Confucianism and Taoism while the genuine intellectuals among them became convinced of the superiority of Buddhist thought. One can understand how in such times the Buddhist idea of salvation in a paradise attracted them. In the last resort the Buddhist monasteries were the only agencies through which the land could be administered, even though the increase in their tax-free lands created its own problems for the national treasuries. The colourful rituals of the church attracted the lower levels of the population, classes for which Confucianism did not cater. Buddhism, with its prohibition of all killing, is essentially a peaceful way of life and the rulers for their part were generally happy to support a religion which kept a population calm. But the steady gains of the faith were not without setbacks – as for example in the persecution of the faith in the north in AD 446.

In return for court support the monks were prepared to represent the rulers as divinities on earth or as examples of the type of enlightened kings celebrated in the scriptures as having helped the faith in India. In short, in a period of disintegration, Buddhism provided society with its only cement and the individual with his only hope for the future both personally and collectively.

The northern invaders capitulated on the one hand to the power of Buddhism and on the other to the achievements of Chinese culture. In the course of a century or so they came quite sincerely to regard themselves as the true inheritors and champions of Han culture. This again set a pattern which later invaders were to follow.

The most important of these northern invaders founded the Northern Wei Dynasty (AD 386-535). The T'o-pa tribe which created it was a mixture of Hsiung-nu (or Hsien-pei) and Turkish nomads with Mongol elements. Only they, by trusting and recruiting their Chinese victims, were able to create a stable régime in north China. Their kings became zealous converts to Buddhist thought in the mid-fifth century. Fired by a devout and inspiring monk they backed the carving of the cave temples of Yün-kang at Ta-t'ung, their early capital near the Great Wall. Here thousands of sculptors laboured for decades to create a number of colossal statues and myriads of smaller ones out of the living rock (*plate* 52). This vast undertaking can compare with any of the world's great religious works of art.

52 View of part of the cave-temples at Yün-kang, Shansi, North China, showing
a colossal Buddha and attendant Bodhisattva carved into the limestone rock of
the cliffs 460-80 AD.

53 Large statue of Sakyamuni, the historical Buddha, at Yün-kang, Shansi. Another standing example of the early style, 460-80 AD, before the indigenous Chinese style asserted itself.

54 Minor statues of two Buddhas in a niche surrounded by a frieze of other Buddhas and worshippers, in the early Yün-kang style, 460-80 AD.

55 Stone figure of a Bodhisattva at Yün-kang, in the late Yün-kang style when it had become fully Chinese. Posture and attributes, *moudras*, or hand gestures, all have particular significance.

56 Part of the main cave-temple at Lung-mên, Honan province, central China, showing large figures of, from l. to r., a Bodhisattva, a guardian and a Heavenly King, in full T'ang dynasty style, 672-5 AD. (Chapter Four and cf plate 90).

When in AD 494 the capital was moved to Loyang, a similar work was started at Lung-mên. Other similar caves had already been started at Tun-huang, the westernmost gateway to China, and were being worked on at the, lately rediscovered, site of Mai-chi-shan where the hundreds of figures span the Northern Wei to the Sung periods. The most important Northern Wei remains at Tun-huang are the wall paintings, some of the earliest in China (see later).

57 Chinese stone Bodhisattva from Lung-men, in typical Late Northern Wei dynasty style with archaic smile, as at Yün-kang (plate 55).

60 Large Chinese gilt bronze figure of Maitreya Buddha (the Buddha of the Future) standing on a lotus pedestal, dated 477 AD. A model of the culmination of the early Northern Wei style, drapery hanging in regular folds with a tendency to cling to the body's form.

The colossal statues at Yün-kang as well as the whole idea of cave temples are of Indian origin, as seen at Bamiyan in Afghanistan. The early style of Yün-kang (*plate* 53) was an extension of the Central Asian oasis styles which in themselves were a combination of native Indian and Hellenised Indian modes.

Within half a century these inherited styles gave way to the linear, geometric style which had been traditional in Chinese art from Han times and before, (*plate* 57). The beauty of the naked body, sensually

71

61 Chinese gilt bronze altarpiece of Buddha attended by Bodhisattvas, priest, and flying angels surrounding the halo. Sixth century AD.

62 Chinese gilt bronze shrine figures of Sakyamuni Buddha accompanied by Prabhūtaratna Buddha, (a Buddha of the Past), dated 518 AD. A bird, an incense burner and a lion-dog support the platform.

expressed in the Indian ideal, disappea
loping rhythmically arranged draperie
falling thickly over the pedestals on w
in the round gave way to a frontal pos
angular with an archaic smile about t
late Northern Wei sculpture is one of
qualities appear in the portable shrines
examples of which have survived.

63 Chinese painted terracotta tomb figure of a caparisoned horse of the Northern Wei dynasty. Sixth century AD. Pottery tomb figures were by now approaching the high degree of naturalism, liveliness and variety to come in the T'ang dynasty. (pp 76-77)

人咸知修其容莫知飾其性性之
不飭或愆禮正斧之澡之尤念作
聖

64 Section of the Chinese scroll 'Admonitions of the Imperial Instructress (to
lady court attendants)' attributed to Ku K'ai-chih (c 344-c 406), now thought
to be a faithful copy by a later painter. Such copying was common and accepted
in a culture that revered tradition so highly. Here elements of the Han style
persist (cf plate 41) within a much more fluid composition. The sections are
separated by lines of calligraphy. (p. 78)

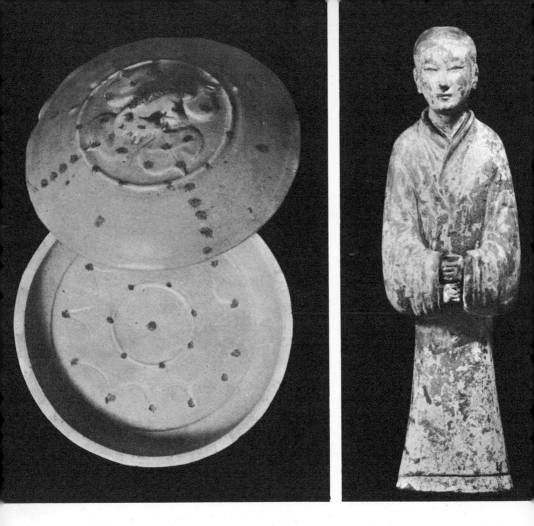

In ceramics, the Yüeh potters continued to produce wares of increasing refinement. The toilet box (*plate* 65) with its comb markings and spots of brown has a sturdy elegance and refined taste which look forward to the great products of the following centuries. Perhaps the most revealing pottery products were the tomb figures which were made in increasing numbers from the end of the Han dynasty onwards. *Plate* 66, a guardian figure of about the third century AD, shows a more developed technique and command of plasticity compared with the Han figures (see *plate* 30). By the fifth-sixth

65 Chinese fourth-sixth century Yüeh type toilet box with iron spots and comb marking and quatrefoil on the lid, a familiar Han motif in simple form.

66 Chinese painted grey pottery tomb figure of an attendant, third century AD. Though still fairly stiff, the fullness and plasticity of this figure is an advance on Han and a precursor of T'ang pottery figures.

67 Chinese stone chimera of the third-fourth century. Dynamic, but angular and linear in approach.

68 Chinese stone chimera of the fifth-sixth century. Integrated into one plastic swirling movement. These mythical creatures lined the approaches to tombs.

century the modellers had achieved remarkable skill, especially in richly caparisoned horses with their heavy bodies, swelling chests, short legs and thick necks (*plate* 63). It is interesting to compare this horse with the T'ang dynasty animal in *plate* 87. In a relatively short space of time the modellers had made a further development to complete mastery of all the secrets of naturalistic representation of movement, a striking contrast to much of the Buddhist sculpture. Looking back, it is illuminating to compare two stone chimera, one from about the third century, the other from the fifth-sixth century (*plates* 67, 68).

They mark the change in approach to sculpture during these centuries – the one is strictly Chinese, the other has inherited the sculptural traditions of the West. Towards the end of the Six Dynasties period foreign influences also began to make themselves felt in the decoration of Yüeh wares.

The Six Dynasties period was one of great literary activity, particularly in the fields of adventure stories and poetry. The poetry in particular abounds in references to landscape and man's reaction to it. Poetry and landscape paintings were to be closely related in the centuries to come but existing paintings of this period are rare. Among the few are the wall paintings at Tun-huang where landscapes are found as backgrounds to Buddhist stories (*plate* 69). Critics in these centuries laid the foundations for what was to grow into a vast library of writings on the art of painting and on paintings themselves, the most famous author being the fifth century writer Hsieh Ho whose tersely formulated Six Principles have given as much cause for argument (especially among translators) as they have provided inspiration for subsequent centuries of painters. In broad outline, his first and most important principle stresses the importance for a painter to create a sense of life, movement and vitality in his works. It is of no small significance that such a theory was developed so early in the long history of Chinese painting.

Some evidence is available of the court painting of this formative period from what is generally believed to be a later but faithful copy of the work of the most eminent painter of the time, Ku K'ai-chih (c. 344-405). The scroll 'Admonitions of the Imperial Instructress' in the British Museum (*plate* 64) is a didactic work in a number of separate scenes intended to show how ladies of noble birth should behave even at the most trying times – as for instance when they lose their favoured position in the Imperial harem! The intense but passionless figures immediately recall the tomb figures of the period in their slim, high-waisted elegance. The painter has used elementary shading (a device introduced from Central Asia) and in places attempted perspective but without great success. However, he had a fine sense of line drawing and the grouping of figures, while his gift for drama and depicting personality is a development in the best Han tradition. The

69 One of the Seven Buddhas of the Past being carried up on five mythical creatures; detail of a temple wall painting in a cave at Tun-huang, in the far west of China, c 500 AD. This very early style with only rudimentary mountain landscape is still very much under western influence.

70 Detail of the side of a Chinese engraved limestone sarcophagus of c 525 AD, depicting the deeds of various paragons of filial piety. Probably a version in stone of a well-known painted scroll, it gives a good idea of early Chinese painted landscape styles now lost. The development of landscape painting is one of the most important aspects of Chinese art. Beginning in the Han dynasty it reached its climax in the Sung.

calm rhythms which one associates with Chinese painting are here already established and we see in its early stages an art which is highly intellectualized and stylized, a form of painting which is severely controlled without being lifeless.

Already Chinese painters had won a relatively exalted place in society and their services were in great demand at the courts. The fame and honour to be gained from painting very soon put the art on a high level and served to inspire painters throughout the centuries.

80

In China, it was generally only painters who gained artistic renown whereas in Japan, where all art is considered to be one, the humbler craftsmen, like potters, lacquerers and certainly sculptors, very often shared the honours.

To see how painters of the time might have managed landscape themes we must turn to such monuments as the early sixth century stone sarcophagus now at Kansas City (*plate* 70). A craftsman has incised on stone slabs scenes illustrating paragons of filial piety. The schematic rock formations, the rhythmically expressed trees, the disposition of men and animals in living landscapes worked into the stone, serve to underline how much we must have lost in works on silk and paper from those early years. We shall see later how the Japanese took up this style (see *plate* 80).

For the earliest surviving religious painting we must go to the Caves of the Thousand Buddhas at Tun-huang in the west of China. Work was started at this frontier site in the second half of the fourth century about a hundred years before the Northern Wei Emperors adopted the Buddhist faith and started the Yün-kang caves. At Tun-huang the caravans from Central Asia first entered China proper. There too the travellers left the safety of their homelands for the dangers of travel to India. It was one of the earliest centres of Buddhist study, an oasis in the desert with nearly five hundred caves hollowed into the soft cliff. The rock was unsuitable for carving and the craftsmen made their statues of clay on a frame and then painted them. This provides opportunities for greater plastic effects and realism (*plate* 71) than stone.

At Tun-huang we have the largest corpus of early Chinese painting that has survived. The site is a provincial one and the quality could not have been up to the standards seen in the capital, but the twenty-two Wei dynasty caves give a brilliant idea of the early figural and landscape painting of China. *Plate* 69 which illustrates an event in one of the previous lives of the Buddha, dates to about AD 500 and again shows the continuation of Han landscape traditions.

In China Buddhism had to compete with the entrenched forces of Confucianism and Taoism. But in Korea and Japan it had no such formidable opponents and its victory was more rapid, more complete and, if not more sincere at least less qualified. What is more important, it provided the vehicle by which Chinese culture was swiftly carried beyond the borders of China itself.

The Chinese military outposts in Korea, weakened by the northern invasions, did not survive beyond the beginning of the fourth century AD. In the period from about the first century BC to the first century AD three states had been emerging in Korea – the first being Koguryo in the northern half of the peninsular, then Silla in the south-east and

82

71 Two painted clay figures, the youngest and eldest disciples of the Buddha, in a cave at Tun-huang, Chinese Turkestan, sixth-seventh century. One of the relatively rare occurences of portraiture in Chinese Buddhist sculpture, an art which was to be highly developed later on in Japanese sculpture.

Paekche in the south-west. A small enclave in the middle of the south coast seems to have had strong connections, probably through blood relations and trading interests, with the emerging Japanese state. During this long Three Kingdoms Period (c. 37 BC - AD 668) contact with China was always maintained to a greater or lesser degree.

In 342 Koguryo in the north was for a time overrun by the Hsien-pei tribe and it must be remembered that the T'o-pa tribe which established the Northern Wei dynasty were a branch of the Hsien-pei. Although the invaders were driven out, the Koguryo still maintained contact with the nomads of north China of that period. The Koguryo probably considered them a lesser evil than the newly rising nomad danger still farther to the north, the Juan-juan tribe. The Northern Wei, for their part, probably found it politic to protect their flank against the Juan-juan by preserving good relations with Koguryo. The official date given for the introduction of Buddhism to Koguryo is 372 AD and throughout the following century Chinese administrative and social ideas steadily gained ground. The art of Koguryo in this period owed much to Han Chinese traditions as can be seen in the fifth and sixth centuries wall paintings of the tombs at T'ung-kou where horsemen at full gallop pursue game or entertainers amuse their lords and ladies (*plate* 51). The tradition is the same as that at Tun-huang.

Paekche in the south-west also looked to China but to the states of the south mainland rather than to the north. At the same time it attempted to ally itself either with Silla or with Japan against the ever threatening Koguryo from the north. The date given for the official introduction of Buddhism there is 384 AD. Its art is perhaps best represented by the Kudara Kannon – Kudara being the Japanese for Paekche. This mysterious, aloof statue, now preserved in Japan, was probably brought from Paekche or made in Japan by a Paekche craftsman. Its sculptural traditions are certainly from a completely different source than those of north China.

Silla, the last state to emerge, had never been occupied by the Chinese nor as strongly influenced by them as the other two states. A strong tribal organisation and rigorous military training enabled it to preserve its independence. A fine gold crown with its antler-like pro-truberances (*plate* 73) immediately reminds one of the antler decorations

72 The Kudara (Japanese for the Korean kingdom of Paekche) Kannon. A painted wood Bodhisattva, either brought from Korea, or, more likely, carved by a Korean craftsman in Japan where it now stands. Sixth-seventh century. An excellent facsimile is in the British Museum.

73 Korean gold crown with antler-like projections and jade pendants, from the kingdom of Silla, fifth-sixth century. The discs glinting would give a probably intended impression of flame from the king's head.

which form a notable and mysterious ingredient of nomad art. Small curved stone pendants called in Japanese *magatama* have been found in both Silla and in Japan and indicate fairly close connections. Chinese thought and institutions were slow to penetrate Silla and Buddhism was established comparatively late, not until AD 528 according to the records. Silla was now ready to begin the process of conquest which was to destroy the independence of first Paekche, then Koguryo and finally to unify the country. What little art remains from the Three Kingdoms period shows strong influences of late Northern Wei sculptural patterns. The pottery is relatively crude, but the tomb figures, despite their heaviness, have a lively humour and show keen observation. It is also particularly interesting to see how Chinese landscape traditions found their echoes in the Korean peninsula (*plate* 76).

74 A Korean earthenware bowl with stamped decoration, eighth-ninth century Silla dynasty. Such wares are crude by Chinese standards.

75 Korean pottery vessel in the form of a mounted warrior, fifth-sixth century Silla dynasty. Although heavily and clumsily modelled by Chinese standards, it has a vitality of almost grand proportions.

76 Korean stamped brick of clay earthenware from the kingdom of Paekche,
seventh century. An example of early Korean landscape art with stylized mountains, trees and clouds. The Chinese version of this style can be seen in plate 70.

Meanwhile, a still more independent, less sinicised nation was emerging in the Japanese islands. The Japanese seem to have had close contacts with the south coast of Korea in the fourth century and a proportion of the ruling class of Japan may well have originated in Korea itself. Japan in fact was always a factor in early Korean alliances. In 400 AD Paekche scribes went to the Japanese court to teach the Japanese how to keep their records in Chinese fashion and Paekche seems to have been the link between China and Japan. Korean immigrants flowed to the islands where their superior knowledge and abilities in many walks of life made them welcome among the most progressive of the Japanese tribes who were always on the look-out for abilities which would give them advantage over kindred tribes. Some of the Korean immigrants must have had established contacts with the old Han military colonies. They found in Japan a country at the end of the Yayoi period in what is known as the Old Tomb period (third-sixth centuries AD), so called from the custom of burying important dead in huge mounds as in Korea (see Chapter Two).

The native religion of Japan at this time has come to be known as Shinto, 'the Way of the Gods'. Fundamentally Shinto is a simple animism, a religion of thankfulness for the bounty and beauty of a kindly nature. Fertility beliefs played a large part in it as in earlier Jōmon thought. Shinto priests, in their function as exorcists and in performing ceremonies of cleansing and ritual abstention, are related to the shamans of Korea and north-east Asia rather than to anything found in China. The deeper rooted attitudes of Shintoism have left a distinguishing mark on Japanese art and sometimes result in fundamental differences from that of China.

In either 552 or 538 AD Paekche presented a gilt bronze image of the Buddha to the Japanese court and historians generally take this event as marking the official introduction of Buddhism to the islands. A semi-political, semi-religious struggle divided the court throughout the sixth century and from this Buddhism emerged supreme. The energetic, adaptable Japanese people also assumed the Chinese system of administration and tried to emulate the achievements of its richer, older neighbour. One can imagine the wonder which the Japanese experienced when their first travellers visited the Chinese mainland.

Although much of this story belongs to the next chapter, some of the early Japanese Buddhist art from the first half of the Asuka period (538-645 AD) was directly inspired by Chinese and Korean works of the period before 600 AD. Pride of place in these early works must be given to the Sakyamuni Triad (Sakyamuni being the historical Buddha), dated AD 623, a large gilt bronze piece in beautiful condition (*plate* 77). Its maker was a Korean Chinese immigrant named Tori whose family came to Japan in 532. The style is obviously that of the late Northern Wei (see *plate* 57) with later modifications, transferred to bronze. The canons of such images were fairly rigidly circumscribed but in the background the artist has produced a swirling pattern which is highly individual. How fortunate we are that the Japanese have so carefully preserved their early works! In Japan, Buddhism has never suffered such persecutions as in China where they lamentably destroyed so much art. The Shinto religion opposed it from time to time but the tendency has been to try to absorb it rather than to crush it, to create a synthesis. Many famous statues were, and some still are, 'secret statues' shown to the public for a few brief hours in the year or even not at all and this has helped to preserve a number of fine early works.

Perhaps the most remarkable thing about the Tori Triad is the fine workmanship. The Japanese have always mastered imported techniques in a very short time, and have sometimes surpassed their teachers, the wood block printing technique being one outstanding example. Part of this characteristic is the Japanese willingness to try their hands at anything – an adventuresomeness and love of experiment which has produced some of Japan's most original products and gives great variety to its craft-products.

The other side of this coin is a deeply-rooted sense of inferiority *vis-à-vis* the overwhelming power of Chinese culture. This at times led to some very sterile copying of things Chinese. From early times Japanese art like Japanese life in general has swayed like a pendulum between its own tradition and foreign innovations. The Japanese have never enjoyed the massive equilibrium of China, the calm sense of cultural superiority which has brought the Chinese through all their vicissitudes.

77 Japanese gilt bronze Sakyamuni triad of 523 AD, called the Tori Triad after the name of its maker, of Korean Chinese origin. (cf plates 57,63).

Another early type of statue, seated in European fashion with one leg crossed on the other and finger to chin in pensive attitude, originated in the Chinese Northern Ch'i Period in the sixth century and from there found its way to Korea and thence to Japan (*plate* 78). Variously identified as a portrait of Sakyamuni or as Maitreya, (the Buddha of the Future, the Buddhist Messiah), it shows a new sense of physical beauty which nothing previously produced leads one to expect. A large Korean gilt bronze example (*plate* 79) from seventh century Silla and in Japan this Maitreya of the Kōryūji, (*plate* 78),

78 Head of a Japanese figure of Sakyamuni or Maitreya (the historical Buddha or the Buddha of the future) mid-seventh century. Inspired by a Korean gilt bronze model (plate 79) this figure is in wood, the material best suited to Japanese craftsmen and in which they surpassed the Chinese.

79 The seventh century Korean gilt bronze seated Buddha which inspired the Japanese figure on plate 78, and which was itself taken from Chinese prototypes in stone (cf plate 57).

could almost have been made by the same hand. The Japanese example, however, is in wood, a material which has always suited best the sculptural talents of the Japanese. Stone is lacking in the islands and wood became the most popular medium. In working wood the Japanese have always surpassed the Chinese.

Another interesting illustration of how the Japanese took over Chinese traditions is seen in the Tamamushi or ' Beetle Wing ' shrine, a name derived from setting iridescent beetles' wings beneath open metalwork, (*plate* 80). The shrine is of lacquered wood and has on its panels figures and illustrations of stories from the past lives of the Buddha. Some have landscape elements which repeat faithfully the conventions seen in early Chinese works such as the Kansas City sarcophagus (*plate* 70). The organization of the scenes and their dramatic sense are very highly developed. Nothing surviving from China can compare with it.

By the end of this period important changes were taking place on the mainland. Absorption into the Chinese pattern did not solve the problem of the T'o-pa. Remnants of the nomads who could not settle to the Chinese way of life led revolts which weakened their strength. The Chinese regained power. One Chinese group established the Northern Ch'i dynasty (557-580) in the west. The traditional pattern of each group seeking allies with rising nomad tribes in the north for their mutual protection continued. The sixth century saw the emergence of the Turks as the most dangerous enemy of the Chinese in the north.

Closer contacts with India, then in the Gupta period, sculpturally one of its greatest, produced new types of sculpture in the sixth century. The body began to acquire life beneath the draperies. Jewellery became rich, elaborate crowns surmount human faces. Instead of Sakyamuni, the historical Buddha, Maitreya, the Buddha of the Future who will return to earth from his paradise to save the world, became increasingly popular. The full impact of this seductive Indian style was felt in the following dynasty — the T'ang (618-907).

80 Painted lacquer panel from the side of the Tama-mushi (Beetle Wing) Shrine in the Honju-ji Monastery, Nara, Japan. It illustrates on a single plane three scenes from the story of a former life of the Buddha in which, out of compassion for all living creatures, he gave his life to feed a starving tigress and her young. Sixth-seventh century AD.

81 Chinese black limestone Bodhisattva of the Northern Ch'i dynasty (557-58 AD), just prior to the T'ang dynasty, showing how bejewelled and ornate Chinese Buddhist sculpture was becoming.

82 T'ang dynasty stone figure of a celestial being from the T'ien-lung-shan cave-temples, Shansi, north China. In it the full influence of the second invasion of Indian sculptural norms (the first came with the introduction of Buddhism) is evident in the diaphanous drapery, indolent posture and appreciation of warm, living flesh. (pp 99 and 101)

CHAPTER FOUR

China unites again
The power of Chinese culture in the T'ang Dynasty
over Great Sillan Korea and Nara Japan

The urge and ambition to unite China and restore it to its former glory had animated almost all the contending states in the centuries following the Han. This long awaited reunification was the achievement of the over-ambitious, short-lived Sui dynasty (AD 589-618). Its excesses and its megalomania were its undoing but it laid the foundations for the glorious T'ang centuries which followed (AD 618-907). The barbarian occupation had not only been a salutary political experience, it had also added a new and vigorous strain to Chinese blood. The Chinese now fully realised that in their dealing with the northerners, attack was the best form of defence. Thus the Sui effected their control over the Turks in the north and the Tibetans and Mongols in the west. Strangely enough, however, their campaigns against the Koguryo in Korea (612-614) ended in defeat.

The founder of the T'ang dynasty had much northern blood. He placed his father on the throne in 618 and ascended it himself in 626 AD. By 624 he had cowed the unruly Turks in the north and by the middle of the century the Chinese controlled the barbarian tribes in the west. Thus the important economic and cultural routes to the west were secure and contact with the outside world through them was to give China of the T'ang Dynasty an abundance of artistic wealth and innovation. Chinese armies, emulating those of the Han, reached to the Oxus valley and Upper Afghanistan. Tibet came under Chinese suzerainty. Emperor Kao Tsung (649-683) even brought the intractable Korean peninsular under Chinese control. He achieved this by alliance with the south-western state of Silla which by 668 had defeated

Koguryo, Paekche and remnants of Japanese forces. The new Silla remained loyal and obedient to T'ang China.

Under Ming Huang (AD 712-756) the T'ang enjoyed the second period of its greatness. In the far west even the militant Arabs were for a while kept at bay. But in 751 the dynasty met with a serious reverse at the hands of the Arabs and, although with the support of its barbarian allies it lasted another 150 years, revolts and internal disruption increasingly weakened it from then onward. Nevertheless, for the first half of the period, the country was ably governed by a strong centralized administration. The economy had been expanding, especially in the south. An efficient bureaucracy, based on Confucian principles and recruited by fair examinations, effectively directed a vast empire. The Chinese civil service of eighth century China was a prodigious political achievement.

The capital at Ch'ang-an, a city with over one million inhabitants within its walls, was the brilliant centre of this empire. Admiring visitors from less developed neighbouring lands would find amidst the temples and palaces people from all over the known world, representatives of every creed and colour. Buddhism became increasingly Chinese in outlook. Various sects, stressing one or another aspect of the faith, gained followings in China and thence spread to Japan. Some stressed secret doctrines and magical formulae, others preached salvation simply by means of calling on the Buddha's name. Yet another, the Ch'an or, as it is known in Japan, the Zen sect, stressed the efficacy of meditation which brought sudden enlightenment. At times the wealth which the monasteries acquired, together with the jealousy which their influence aroused in Confucians and Taoists alike, brought persecutions, but generally speaking this was the great age of Buddhism. The faith reached a height of influence and artistic inspiration which it never again achieved.

In literature, the poetry of a galaxy of writers enriched not only the Chinese but, in translation, the poetic thought of the whole world. Society was wealthy, the towns prosperous, life highly sophisticated. The quantity and quality of artistic output, even as it has survived after more than a thousand years, reflects these aspects of T'ang life. The brilliance of T'ang civilization acted as a magnet and as an

83 Chinese wooden head of the Bodhisattva Avalokitesvara (Ch. Kuan-yin), later to turn into a female deity known as the ' Goddess of Compassion and Mercy '. (see plate 132)

example to all the other civilizations of the Far East. They strove to emulate Chinese institutions (often with dangerous modifications) and to copy its culture whatever the cost. What Greece and Rome were to the West, China was to the East.

Religious sculpture shows an immediate change. Now that the routes to the west were secure, the Chinese re-established their direct contacts with India. The sculptors, as recently as the short-lived Sui dynasty still making relatively unimpassioned and static icons, were now completely captivated by the seductive sensuality of Indian plastic ideals. Deities were now no longer enigmatic, spiritual figures in full draperies but desirable human beings sculpted fully in the round and with positive enjoyment of the flesh. Draperies became thin or

84, 85, 86 Three examples of Chinese T'ang Dynasty (618-907) naturalistic modelling: a small gilt bronze figure, a large stone torso and a glazed pottery animal, all imbued with a new sense of life and movement.

non-existent, the jewellery ornate. The figures bend and sway in easy indolence. The movement, the living quality demanded of painting seems also to have become a canon of the sculptor's art. In clay sculpture the T'ang artists also showed their complete mastery of the expression of dynamic plastic forms (*plate* 86).

To appreciate the full achievement of T'ang sculpture we must travel quickly further east to Japan where T'ang inspired treasures have been preserved far better than on the mainland itself. The Japanese were not content for long to accept their ideas of Buddhism second-hand via Korea and they early began to travel to the Chinese capital. What they brought back with them inspired the nascent Japanese state to a tremendous effort of emulation. That they achieved

87 Chinese life-sized grey limestone panel in deep relief of one of the horses belonging to the T'ang emperor, T'ai Tsung, from his tomb built in 637. This early T'ang horse is a monumental version of the freer styles in pottery.

88 This more than life sized gilt bronze Bodhisattva shows how rapidly and closely T'ang styles were reproduced in Japan (cf plates 82, 84, 85), where they are better preserved than in China. This has been called the finest T'ang bronze figure which has survived.

so much in such a short time is a tribute to the energy and imagination of this relatively backward people. Cities were built in Chinese style, Chinese manners and modes became the standards of civilised behaviour. The Early Nara (sometimes called Tempyo) Period (AD 645-712) and the Late Nara (or Hakuho) Period (712-94) united Chinese inspiration with Japanese craftsmanship. The bronze Bodhisattva in *plate* 88 has been called the finest T'ang sculpture to have survived. Many such figures must have been made in China, but they have subsequently been lost or melted down for their metal value. In Japan, where Buddhism was never persecuted and its following has supported it more faithfully, the temples have played a larger part in life than in China. The Japanese themselves have always had a greater respect for their treasures than the prodigal Chinese with the result that a remarkably large proportion of great religious monuments have survived. The Bodhisattva on *plate* 88, one figure of a trinity, has monumentality

102

89 Eighth century Japanese painted clay figure, probably of Gakko (Moonlight) Bodhisattva. The eastern interpretation of the Indian Brahma-deva, supreme god, creator of all things, who was early incorporated into Buddhism. A figure of the utmost spirituality.

and grandeur allied to an almost overpowering humanity, the hallmark of T'ang art.

In clay, large figures have survived over a thousand years, almost miraculously considering the fragility of the material. Here the Japanese skill in reproducing textures and their love of fine surfaces seems to surpass anything we have from the China of that day. The divine beings they portray are sincere and uncomplicated religious idols, saintly human beings secure and serene in their conviction of the absolute goodness of their faith. Their faces are almost portraits. They are the perfection of what the provincial site of Tun-huang revealed in coarser grain.

The T'ang Chinese *lokapala*, or 'guardian', ready to strike down the evil-doer was a mass produced article for burial with the pious dead. The idea finds nobler expression in the powerful large figures of the Japanese Todai-ji temple (*plate* 90) and in observing this one

103

90 Large Japanese painted clay figure of a *lokapala* or guardian of the Buddhist faith, eighth century, in the Todai-ji, Nara. Such figures must have existed in T'ang China, though none have survived other than duller, provincial versions.

91 Japanese dry lacquer portrait of the priest Ganjin, who was one of the early Buddhist missionaries from China to Japan and lost his sight on the journey. Made soon after his death in 763, this is one of the most moving of many fine portraits, a speciality of Japanese sculpture.

is driven to wonder what splendid works of T'ang dynasty China, alas, have not survived the turbulent centuries — the rise and fall of dynasties, the jealousies of the Confucians, and the withering of the faith! As with clay, so also with the rare technique of sculpture in dry lacquer. A few fragments have survived from China but in Japan the technique was used to brilliant effect to produce some of the most moving of all early Far Eastern sculpture (*plate* 91).

By going to Japan to see some of the finest T'ang sculpture we have by-passed Korea and we must now look for a moment at the impact T'ang China had on that peninsula. When China re-united in 589, the Sui emperors reverted to the traditional Chinese policy *vis-à-vis* their northern enemies (this time the Turks) and tried to outflank them. But, as has already been mentioned, the Sui met with little success in Korea and the only effect of T'ang intervention was to

105

92 High relief granite figure of an eighth century Bodhisattva at the Korean cave-temple of Sokkul-am, showing strong T'ang Chinese influence. (cf plates 82, 84, 85)

help Silla defeat its northern rivals, Paekche (660-663) and then Koguryo (668). The Koreans under Silla steadfastly refused to accept direct Chinese control and Silla, although paying tribute, remained technically independent. Nevertheless as in Japan what Chinese armies and diplomacy failed to accomplish Chinese culture achieved, and Silla was completely under Chinese cultural influence, independent only in name.

After the unification of the country in 668, Korea remained united for almost all the following centuries. The emulation of Chinese cultural patterns, again as in Japan, did, of course, undergo some modification, for better or for worse. For example, whereas in China the civil service examinations were broadly based, in Korea and Japan recruitment was restricted to the nobility. Moreover, Confucianism, the philosophical basis of the Chinese administrative class, made little appeal to both Koreans and Japanese. It was always Buddhism, especially in its simpler, more optimistic and even magical aspects, which attracted the peoples outside China proper. Eminent monks travelled between the two kingdoms bringing each new sect to Korea. But the Chinese language and literary forms did capture the educated classes, and trade was a vigorous and an important element in the flow of culture.

The art of this 'Great Silla' period was centred at the capital, Kyongju, but a sixteenth century Japanese invasion destroyed many of its relics. The contents and ruins of Pulguk-sa Monastery outside the city and the cave-temple of Sokkul-am on a hillside behind the monastery give a fine idea of the achievements of this T'ang inspired art. The cave-temple has now been restored to much of its original condition and the granite bas-reliefs it contains are among the finest examples of early Buddhist art. The huge Buddha, Bodhisattvas, heavenly kings and arhats dating from probably 751 all show the typical T'ang full-bodied, swaying, bejewelled and draped figures familiar from sites in China proper like Lung-mên. It is difficult, if not impossible, to distinguish any exclusively Korean features in this sculpture. If anything the Korean approach is somewhat more discreet than the Chinese treatment and the bodies are treated with slightly less sensuality, whereas the surfaces and their decoration are lingered over

93 Detail of the Chinese scroll 'Ladies Playing Double Sixes' in ink and colour on silk attributed to Chou Fang (active c 780-804). Figures similar to these occur in clay tomb models of the period. (pp 108/9).

94 Detail from a long Chinese scroll of portraits of emperors in ink and colour on silk attributed to Yen Li-pên (died 673). This, like plate 93, is in the mainstream of T'ang painting — landscape, bird and flower painting were not taken up fully until the Sung dynasty.

with greater care and delicacy. The hands in particular have an exaggerated grace which the Japanese took up to great effect.

The leadership of China was stronger in painting than even in sculpture. Portrait painting was one of the preoccupations of the Chinese court and skilled artists like Yen Li-pên were assured of a comfortable living. In fact most of the outstanding painters of the time were attracted by the rewards of court service. The cosmopolitan life of Ch'ang-an provided ample material for them – just as it

96 Detail of the head of the Goddess of Compassion from the wall paintings in the Honju-ji, Nara, Japan, of the mid-seventh century, showing the farthest eastern extension of an international style, its penultimate link being metropolitan China.

In Buddhist painting, compositions became larger and far more complicated than in the Northern Wei period. Scenes from Buddhist histories appear side by side with grandiose representations of Buddhist paradises. The temples of the big cities did not survive the persecutions and the passing of centuries but at Tun-huang enough remains to show the technical advances which the painters had made and the way in which they had incorporated Indian, Iranian and Chinese elements into an harmonious whole. As with sculpture, we must rely upon what the Japanese have preserved for an idea of the finest T'ang wall painting. The Hōryū-ji Monastery near Nara contained fine examples of metropolitan style Buddhist wall paintings (*plate* 96). We are unlikely ever to discover whether they were from the hand of a Chinese, Korean or Japanese painter but they represent the farthest eastern extension of a style which stretched from Central Asia to Japan. The outlines are firm, the modelling well-defined, the poses sensual but restrained. The religious art of T'ang shares the richness, complexity, assurance and outgiving of its secular art. The destruction of these wall-paintings by fire in 1949 was a tremendous loss.

Finally in painting, the late T'ang is credited with originating the art of pure landscape painting in ink. As perfected some centuries later this is one of the greatest contributions of Chinese art to that of the world. Wang Wei (699-759), equally famous for his lyric poetry as for his painting, became a model for later generations of aspiring landscapists.

To the other peoples of the Far East the products of China's craftsmen must have set a new standard in elegance and luxury. Its ceramics remained far in advance of anything not only in Korea and Japan but also anywhere else in the world. To the Han dynasty's green glaze and the olive brown Yüeh wares the T'ang potters now added

97 Part of a Chinese horizontal scroll in ink and colour on paper after the style of the late T'ang poet and painter Wang Wei (699-759), the first Chinese pure landscape painter known.

98 Chinese covered jar with a bright orange-brown glaze introduced in the T'ang dynasty. Its shape is also essentially T'ang (cf plates 99, 103, 116) Note too the way the glaze has run just short of the bottom of the jar, another T'ang characteristic, which is often more emphasised; it illustrates the T'ang potter's spontaneity and unwillingness to disguise the nature of his materials and workmanship.

cream and a warm orange brown (*plate* 98) to produce the famous 'three-colour' wares. This they applied in a number of variations to a vastly enlarged repertoire of shapes which combine strength and elegance in a manner which is characteristic of the period. Even cobalt blue, imported from the west, was used, sometimes alone. The material of the bodies is more refined than hitherto and often near white. Convention or taste dictated that the lower parts of a pot should

99, 100, 101, 102 Four examples of T'ang dynasty glazed pottery — a bottle and two impressed motif dishes in the newly introduced three-colour glaze, and a large globular bowl in an unusual mottled grey and blue glaze.

often be left bare with the glaze running down in cascades, but stopping short at various distances from the base. Western shapes and decorative motifs, especially those of Sassanian Persia, influenced Chinese potters of the time. Examples of three-colour wares are found in the Shōsō-in, the Japanese repository of Imperial household objects created in 756. There is evidence that the Japanese copied the Chinese three-colour wares and so adept were they that it is impossible to distinguish between the Chinese product and what the Japanese claim is their own.

103/4 Two T'ang Chinese fusions of western influences in a cream glazed amphora of white earthenware and a three-colour glazed ewer. The amphora has dragon handles probably taken from imports of Syrian pots in European glassware designs; the ewer has a bird-head of probable Mediterranean origin, the 'Parthian shot' motif (cf plate 51) and the shape of Sassanian metal ewers.

105 Jar with cover in two-colour glaze, identical with T'ang Chinese wares. Once thought to be Chinese imports, such pieces now appear to be Japanese high class copies of that period.

The culminating achievement of late T'ang ceramics was the invention at about the turn of the tenth century of pure porcelain – over seven hundred years before the West discovered the secret. This was the outcome of using a white firing clay called *kaolin* (from the place where it was dug) allied to centuries of experience with high firing techniques. The creamy white glazes of these pieces combined with perfect ceramic shapes would be hard to surpass (*plate* 116).

The custom of burying with the dead models of people and objects which might usefully serve in afterlife expanded tremendously in T'ang

106 T'ang Chinese glazed pottery tomb figures of a camel and its attendant, the means whereby so many of the world's treasures were brought to China.

107 T'ang Chinese glazed pottery tomb model of traders with their bullock cart. Figures of all nationalities of Central Asia and the Near and Middle East occur in these models.

times. Servants, dancing girls, guards, dwarfs, horses and camels, all the paraphernalia of T'ang life, found still and miniature reflection in the clay figures. Though without doubt they were cheap and were produced in their thousands, a surprising proportion are little masterpieces of sensitive modelling and accurate observations. What a rich picture they give of the life of well-to-do T'ang society, embroidered by what we can today share of the splendour of its textiles, its mirrors, their backs inlaid with mother-of-pearl or silver or the head-dresses of the court ladies (*plates* 108-112).

The Shōsō-in, with its thousands of objects untouched over the centuries, stands as a testimony to the influences of China over Japan. Most of the objects in this sinophile court were Chinese made and

108 T'ang dynasty Chinese bronze mirror back decorated in silver with typical motifs of birds in foliage scrolls. The traditional quatrefoil (cf plate 65) may be seen here elaborated into a floral design like the medallions on many T'ang pots.

imported to serve the Japanese Imperial household. They included mirrors, glass, musical instruments whose sounding boards are covered with brocades worked into fantastic landscapes, screens showing court beauties of Chinese type familiar from T'ang tomb figures, lacquerwork and textiles. In the latter, Persian Sassanian influences are strong, stronger perhaps than in pottery or any of the other art forms and a further indication of the catholicity of T'ang society's taste.

Nothing better illustrates both the luxury and international quality of T'ang culture than its gold and silver work. These precious metals had, of course, been recognised and used for centuries but hitherto works in these mediums had been based on bronze prototypes. Henceforth the craftsmen used them in new shapes and methods of their own right. As a result of the conquest of Persia by Islam many Persian craftsmen fled to China where they were welcome. They and their students produced bowls, cups, stem-cups, figures and ornaments, especially for the hair, and many other objects in cast or beaten silver

109 Chinese T'ang dynasty gold headdress in the form of a peacock, the tail in the never entirely abstract floral designs at which the Chinese excelled.

decorated with incised designs ranging from hunting scenes to graceful floral designs. Naturalistic animals and birds are sometimes cleverly combined with formalized floral motifs in a most elegant manner which foreshadows the graceful incising of later porcelain. The chased design of floral sprays on *plate* 113 stands out clearly against the smooth background. It is easy to understand how such vessels were sought after by those peoples on the outskirts of Chinese civilization for whom T'ang sumptuary art must have been the essence of luxury!

Most historians agree that the revolt of the 'barbarian' Turkish leader An Lu-shan in 755 began the decline of the T'ang. The revolt was put down with the help of other 'barbarian' troops, but from that time the central government was never able to control the generals in the provinces. The empire was under constant attack from north and west. Eunuch influence, as in late Han times, caused growing friction in the capital. Nevertheless, China continued to be relatively prosperous and peaceful for a century and a half. Not until the end of the ninth century did economic conditions become so bad that the peasantry was driven to revolt. The last thirty years until the official end of the dynasty in 907 were marked by risings and by the quarrels of the generals who put them down.

The pattern of events in Korea was strangely similar for here too after the mid-eighth century the prosperity and vigour of Great Silla rapidly declined. The vitality which had enabled Silla to unite the country was not sufficient to administer it. Contact with China weakened the virile foundation of its organisation and since, like Japan, they ignored the recruitment of talent by a broadly based examination system they were left without a strong administration.

110, 111 T'ang dynasty Chinese painted clay tomb figures of two female dancers and opposite, an actress. The subjects and the care given to making each one of the figures found in T'ang tombs give a vivid insight into the quality of the living society that produced them. (p 119)

The country continued for 150 years until the familiar peasant uprising brought about its final collapse in 918.

Meanwhile in Japan the momentous decision to move the capital was made and a completely new city was built and named Kyoto. The Emperor moved there in 793, perhaps glad to escape from the influence of the Nara clergy. There followed what art historians call the Early Heian Period (794-876) which is sometimes again divided into Kōnin (810-23) and Jōgan (859-76). The dominant artistic influence of the time was still Chinese and Buddhist but now two important new sects dominated the arts, the Tendai (Chinese: T'ien-t'ai) and the Shingon (Chinese: Chên-yen). Shingon in particular, an

112 T'ang Chinese embroidered silk, again with a floral motif that is abstracted while giving due attention to the detail of actual flower subjects — a Chinese characteristic, the Japanese would abstract more. (p 120)

113 Chinese T'ang dynasty silver and parcel gilt bowls and covers. The lobed bowl shape is found in T'ang pottery, but the resurgence and skill of T'ang metalwork is greatly due to immigrant Persian craftsmen. (pp 120/1)

esoteric, magical system based ultimately on Indian Tantric beliefs, introduced into Japanese Buddhist thought and art a new element of magic and mystery. The icons became abstruse and either hidden from the view of the general worshipper or understandable only by the trained clergy.

In sculpture the straightforward appeal of the earlier statues was lost. Forms became heavy with symbolic meaning and divorced from reality – heavy overpowering and sensuous. Painting likewise, better adapted than sculpture to complicated iconography, became esoteric in nature and map-like cosmologies were a favourite subject for religious painters. Many of these *mandalas* are saved from dullness by remarkably fine line drawing and their handsome embellishments in gold and silver.

The T'ang period in China had died an ignoble death but its artistic influence continued in the Liao empire of the north. This empire had slowly gained strength during the T'ang period and was created

124

by the Khitan people from south-east Mongolia allied with Manchurian and Korean tribes. During two centuries from 907 they built up and controlled a huge empire from the sea to Central Asia and down to north of the Yellow River with their capital at Peking. They grew fat from trade with and tribute from China and were finally displaced by one of their ruder vassals, the Jürched in 1125. Here in the north the portrait traditions of T'ang continued at their finest and a series of large figures of lohans in typical T'ang three-coloured glazes has survived (see *plate* 131). Technically they are masterpieces, artistically they have an immediate, personal impact, religiously they reflect a belief in an all embracing personal salvation. They are noble and fitting latter-day tributes to what was one of the great periods of mankind.

114 Japanese wood sculpture of Nyoin Kannon, ' The Bodhisattva of Compassion with the gem and the wheel which satisfy all desires.' A secret statue probably made 826-36 epitomizing the solemn dignity and sensuous feelings of mystical Buddhism. (pp 123/4)

115 Blue Fudō — painting on silk of one of the Five Great Kings supposed to protect the Buddhist world. An outstanding example of the terrifying aspects of the new Japanese Buddhism which flourished in the Early Heian period, 794-876 AD.

CHAPTER FIVE

The East Divided
The Fujiwara in Japan

The period (907-960) following the fall of the T'ang dynasty is known as the Five Dynasties. In fact, in the north of China alone there were five successive dynasties while in the south there were no less than another ten but they all controlled only parts of the former empire. On the whole the south fared better than the north because its generals had gained a large measure of independence during late T'ang and they were able to avoid the economic harship caused in the north by constant fighting with barbarian invaders.

While the Southern Kingdoms were only threatened by fellow Chinese to the north, the northeners had to defend themselves against fiercer peoples pressing down upon them. Particularly dangerous were the Khitans who had organized themselves into a centralised military power. The major ethnic group in these northern dynasties was that of the Turks who had played an important role in the destruction of the T'ang, but like other barbarians before them they were themselves unable to administer without corruption or to secure the loyalty of Chinese who might have done it for them.

These fifty-five years may present a sad political picture but they saw cultural and artistic innovations of the greatest importance.

The progress of the great Chinese ceramic craft always seems to have ignored the political disasters which from time to time afflicted the country. Towards the end of the T'ang dynasty the Chinese had discovered the secret of the manufacture of porcelain, and there seems little doubt that in the present period the manufacture of white porcelain wares was stepped up to a considerable quantity and they

116 A Chinese cup and vase of late T'ang dynasty white ware — the first
pure porcelain produced, c 900 AD. (p 117)

were even exported to lands as far distant as the Middle East. Their
simple shapes, models of ceramic perfection, were to reach the height
of their popularity in the coming Sung dynasty.

During the tenth century also the Yüeh wares reached their culmination (*plate* 117) and they too were highly sought after throughout
China and the countries in contact with China. They were so highly
regarded that they ranked as a tribute article. The industry was
centred in the state of Wu-Yüeh (independent until 978 and governed
from its capital at Hangchou). It must have been highly organized and
on a large scale for pieces of the ware have been found in many places
from Japan to the Middle East. With the fall of this independent state
the potteries seem to have declined rapidly, their place being taken
by the products of the kilns of K'aifêng and Lung-ch'üan (see later).

The period was even more important in the field of painting, the
most highly regarded art of China. Here political decadence had a

direct influence. The professional painters who in the T'ang centuries had been assured of a good living could only serve the local leaders in the south where the important custom of imperial patronage survived. The educated administrators, the poets and literateurs found political life too dangerous and many sought refuge in retirement, where they were forced, as in the post-Han period, to re-examine the world in which they lived and the basis of their culture. Among them were a number of very important painters, and the major contribution of these troubled years was certainly in the field of landscape painting.

We have seen how the Chinese love of landscape had slowly been finding individual ways of pictorial expression in the late T'ang dynasty. Wang Wei created a type of pure landscape painting which was to

117 Large jar or amphora (cf plate 103) with incised lotus design and lid with knob in the form of two kissing doves. This tenth century Chinese Yüeh ware is the culmination of thirteen centuries of development of celadons starting in the third century BC (see plates 32, 33). Incised floral motifs became a strong characteristic of Sung dynasty wares (cf plates 120, 121, 125).

become the increasing preoccupation of Chinese artists. It is significant that he was equally a poet, for Chinese literature and poetry for at least a thousand years had been reflecting in the most sensitive way the beauties, the changes, the mood and power of nature. T'ang poetry abounds in the most evocative descriptions of natural scenery and these poems were the intellectual currency of intelligent men in the succeeding centuries. Kuo Hsi, writing in the mid-eleventh century, exclaims how the countryside should nourish a man's nature, how he should delight in the play of rocks and streams, the haze and the mists, the haunting spirits of the mountains. Chinese painters discovered that just with ink and brush they could recreate the grandeur of the world around them and the emotions it aroused inside them.

The spirit of the landscape painters of the mid-tenth century is summarized in the work of the monk Chü-jan. Like a complicated Buddhist iconographical painting, his landscapes (*plate* 118) fill the canvas in a unified whole in which no one part predominates. They overwhelm the senses as does a full symphony orchestra. Man is in true scale, the mountains have an almost god-like grandeur. His vision results from a combination of the possibilities of brush, ink and artistic humility in face of supra-human forces. It is strong, austere and atmospheric, without being outwardly emotional. Such examples of other-wordliness and detachment were to create and inspire the landscape art of China during the following eight centuries.

In Korea the Great Silla period came to an end in 918, only ten years after the fall of T'ang. After over a century of decreasing vitality in the ruling class and increasing economic hardship among the peasants, the country split into three states, Later Paekche, Later Koguryo and Silla. A Koguryo leader named Wang Kon shortened the name of his state to Koryō and established its capital on the west coast at Kaesong. He received the submission of the last King of Silla in 935 and put down the rebellious Paekche in the following year thus uniting the country once again and establishing a dynasty which lasted from 918 to 1392. The brief period between dynasties greatly resembled the Chinese Five Dynasties period. It is not possible to show here what art was produced in this short period. The very great achievement of Koryō will be discussed in the following chapter.

118 ' Seeking the Tao (Way) in the Autumn Mountains ' attributed to Chü-jan (tenth century) in ink on silk. This type of landscape was the inspiration for later Chinese scholar landscape painters. It was a deliberated definition of man's relationship with nature. No one point commands the whole painting, several eye levels and the upward winding path induce one to move through, 'read', the landscape.

However, in Japan more momentous changes were taking place. China, in the throes of the last T'ang century and what followed, no longer presented an example to be followed. Secure in their splendid new capital at Kyoto the Japanese felt themselves increasingly arbiters of their own destiny. The Japanese aristocracy had never allowed the egalitarian Chinese system to threaten its power. The nobles were not sympathetic to a system which could envisage the eclipse of an emperor, so behind the façade of imperial authority the Fujiwara clan exercised political power. Other events in China may have influenced the Japanese. For instance the persecution of Buddhism in China in the mid-ninth century may well have shocked the Japanese and in particular the entrenched monks in the monasteries of Kyoto and Nara. Regular embassies to China stopped in 894. Japan was ready to free itself for the first time from the cultural apron strings of China and produce an art which was far more independent than anything they had hitherto aspired to. The Late Heian Period (897-1185) is sometimes called the Fujiwara Period from the name of this powerful family, and it spanned the Chinese Five Dynasties Period (907-960) and the first half of the Sung period (960-1126).

The new art was centred on the court, where tastes ran more to luxury and refinement than to the rigours of Buddhist sanctions. No society in the history of civilization ever wrapped itself in such exquisiteness. No court was ever more preoccupied with art, beauty, love and intrigue. Even Buddhism reflected this new sentiment. The Amida cult with its vision of the Buddha of the Western Paradise welcoming the faithful to his beautiful Pure Land captured the imagination of populace and painter alike. Not only were paintings of this made but even temples like the Byōdō-in were constructed to reflect as closely as possible on earth the beauties of the Western Paradise. But beneath the light-hearted hedonism of the age ran a strong current of melancholy, an inner sadness that has always been a peculiarly Japanese characteristic.

The spokesman in sculpture for this new sentiment was Jōchō even though he died in 1057, nearly a century after the Sung dynasty had begun. His Amida (*plate* 119) in the Byōdō-in exemplifies the grace and elegance of Fujiwara ideals. The heavy bodies and stiff

119 The Amida Buddha in wood gilt, by the Japanese sculptor Jōchō (died 1057). Unlike earlier statues it was made of a number of separate pieces which were then assembled and finished by the master. This is the model for countless later Buddha figures.

drapery of the previous period are here modified, lightened and humanised. Behind the figure rises a richly carved nimbus. Jōchō and his followers developed a new technique of sculpture-making which was necessary both to satisfy their own desire for finesse and to meet the increasing demand for religious statuary. Instead of using single blocks of wood, they used many smaller pieces which they assembled, probably in the rough, and then added the finishing touches. Thus pupils could learn the craft and increase output while the master was free to apply his talents to the nearly finished figure. The sculptors in this period often enriched the surfaces of their statues (as also their paintings) by a native Japanese technique called *kiri-kane*, 'cut-gold', in which they cut very thin strips of gold leaf and applied them to simulate rich textile designs. The result in sculpture of this attention to detail, decorated surface and love of prettiness was elegant deities within ornate settings which were often more akin to painting than sculpture. The esoteric Buddhist sects concentrated on the production of painted *mandalas* – involved map-like representations of Buddhist cosmologies, or of terrifying 'Enlightened Kings' (*Myō-ō*) designed to deter the evil doer. They must have been particularly effective when seen by the congregation through the flickering lights of altar fires. The variety of services which these sects practised demanded a very wide range of icons and they found that painting met this demand better than sculpture. It was easier too for them to preserve the mystery of these forbidding paintings by keeping them in secrecy (as some still are kept). Their precision of workmanship and the rich surfaces reveal the Japanese hand but as soon as the Sung dynasty had established itself Chinese influences quickly began to re-assert themselves. The more one considers Fujiwara art, the more one wonders how complete in fact was the divorce from China.

Of considerable significance for the future of Japanese arts and crafts was the emergence of the craftsman as a man of social consequence. Apart from painting this never happened in China and its effect on the arts of Japan was to be far-reaching. Japanese artists, sculptors, painters, potters and metal workers obtained far greater independence and became leaders within their own spheres in a way quite unknown in China. This is partly responsible for the rich diversity of later Japanese art.

Hitherto in Japan a peculiar snobbism had compelled artists to paint almost exclusively in the Chinese style (*Kara-e*), even down to imitating imaginary Chinese landscapes. The Japanese were now brought to see the beauties of their own more gentle scenery. The basic ingredients were inherited from the highly coloured T'ang styles but Japanese elements increasingly intrude especially in the famous Japanese *e-makimono* or painted handscrolls which illustrate in most individual ways stories taken from their own history and legend. This is the *Yamato-e* or Japanese painting as opposed to the *Kara-e* or Chinese styles. Its great flowering was to come in the next period, the Kamakura, 1185-1337.

CHAPTER SIX

Three Great Periods: the Sung Dynasty in China, the Koryō Dynasty in Korea, and the Kamakura Dictatorship in Japan

The short periods of disunity in China and Korea were the prelude to what many consider the greatest periods in the arts of both these countries.

The founder of the Sung dynasty seemed at first little more than another military adventurer like his predecessors but his wise and clement administration established the dynasty firmly. He centralised the political, administrative and military powers and set an example of frugality which was all that a good Confucian could ask of an emperor. The perfected examination system, although somewhat narrow in syllabus, provided a stream of first class administrators who were also men of culture and learning. For one hundred years during which the capital was at K'ai-fêng the Sung were prosperous and the country at peace. In 1126 the Sung lost the northern part of their land to invading northerners, the Khitans, and thereafter survived only in the south under increasing pressure, administering a truncated kingdom from their beautiful lakeside capital at Hang-chou.

The peaceful, introspective outlook of the country during this period had its political drawbacks. The Sung were never able to control the traditional enemies in the north by an aggressive policy (the only effective means to contain them), and were forced to resort to the ineffective method of bribery. As a result they were never secure. In the west the barbarian tribes cut off China from the cultural influences which had invigorated the T'ang. Shut in on themselves, the Sung developed a truly Chinese culture. Antiquarianism and an interest in archeaology led to archaism especially in bronze and jade, but other arts experienced a mature flowering of incomparable splendour.

135

120, 121, 122, 123 Chinese Sung dynasty wares and shapes. On this page, a white *ting* ware bird-headed ewer (cf plate 104) and a bowl and toilet box of *ch'ing-pai* (or *ying-ch'ing*) ware, both incised. Opposite, a tea or wine pot of white *ting* ware — developed from T'ang white wares (plate 116) — and a large jar of Tz'u-chou ware with painted decoration.

The porcelain of the period is both technically and artistically the finest the world has produced. The discoveries of the late T'ang were carried to perfection. Porcelain became more refined, the shapes more delicate, the glazes more varied and subtle than anything produced before. The creamy white *ting* wares (*plate* 122), developed from the white wares of the T'ang, now became very thin and translucent with a gentle glaze decorated with free-hand incising or with impressed patterns. The *chün* (*plate* 124) was a new type characterized by a thick deep lavender glaze to which random purple splashes were often added. *Chien* ware (*plates* 126, 194) from Honan or Fukien was a type often reserved for tea bowls, very discreet works, often decorated with inconspicuous hare's fur, oil spot or other markings. A very popular ware, very thin and with the palest of blue glazes, is known as *ying-ch'ing* (*plate* 121) or more recently, after Sir Percival David, as

124, 125 Chinese Sung dynasty wares: a bowl and jar of *chün* ware, a heavy type with thick glaze, and a Northen celadon bowl with free, incised decoration (cf plate 117) and olive green glaze turning dark green where it thickens round the elements of the design.

126 Chinese Sung dynasty large vase of dark brown *chien* ware with lighter brown glazed floral sprays. This ware became very popular in Japan where it was called *temmoku*, a name by which the dark glaze is now more commonly known. (see plate 194 and p 200)

ch'ing-pai, 'blue-white', ware. Shapes are often flower-like and of great sensitivity — one stands amazed that such delicate workmanship has survived the centuries. In Tz'u-chou and its environs was produced a virile type of stone ware for household use which is distinguished by its freehand decoration of supreme confidence, generally in brown or black on white. This is folk-art at its highest.

When the Yüeh kilns ceased production of celadon was taken over by a number of kilns producing what is loosely known as Northern celadon (*plate* 125). Later, the kilns of Lung-ch'üan further south

127 Chinese Sung dynasty vase with bird neck-and-head handle of the finest celadon from the Lung-Ch'üan kilns.

128 Chinese Sung dynasty bowl in *kuan* ware — a crackle-glaze ware that was frequently copied later, in the Ch'ing dynasty. (plate 210)

began to produce the pale green wares (*plate* 127) which found favour not only with the Chinese but also widely throughout the Middle East. They were the first Chinese wares to reach Europe. The Chinese potters also mastered the art of crazing or crackle in glazes and produced some most beautiful effects by this means – especially in a type called *kuan* or 'official' wares. The rarest of all Sung wares, the *ju*, was made for only a few years in the north (*plate* 130).

The first people to press the Sung down from the north were the Khitans who had established an empire in Inner Mongolia as early as 916. From 1004 it included Northern Hopei and had its southern capital at Peking. In all they controlled sixteen prefectures and established in the north a culture of mixed nomad and Chinese elements. The dynasty they established is known as the Liao. They accepted many Chinese institutions including Confucianism but were also

140

129 Chinese vase glazed in green of the Liao dynasty in the north where the traditions of T'ang dynasty pottery persisted, but a number of new shapes were introduced.

devout Buddhists and many repairs were carried out to the Yün-kang temples at this time though often not in the best of taste. The Liao Dynasty was finally swept away by one of their vassals, the Tungusic Jürched, who established the Chin dynasty (1122-1234). The Sung had aided the Jürched to oust their rivals the Khitan but when the Jürched took over the northern areas they continued to expand south at the expense of their erstwhile Chinese allies and captured the Northern Sung capital at K'aifeng in 1126 together with the Chinese Emperor. From this time the Sung hung on somewhat wistfully to their former glories.

Finally both Sung and Chin were swept away by the most devastating of all the barbarian invaders – the Mongols.

The pottery of the Liao peoples was directly inspired by T'ang wares. A white ware has been found in which some of the shapes are

141

130 Vase in the rarest of Sung Chinese wares, the *ju* (p 140). Comparing this with plates 100 or 98 readily shows the difference between T'ang and Sung pottery standards. T'ang pieces show more dramatic changes in their shape, leave the markings of the potter undisguised and stand sturdily. The Sung smooth out their shapes and glazes, stand more delicately and turn T'ang virility into elegance.

distinctive – notably a leather bottle shape and an amphora with very narrow neck and wide mouth. Coloured wares generally have a red or buff body, covered with a white slip and finally glazed. Green is the most frequent colour. Other types had incised decoration in the body under the glaze and yet others applied medallions. Outstanding is a series of almost life-size lohans, technical and artistic masterpieces (*plate* 131). It is interesting to see how by this time the Northerners' artistic traditions had become almost entirely sinicised.

Sculpture, once direct contacts with India were broken, quickly reverted to Chinese norms. The best known of Sung Buddhist sculptures are the indolent *Kuan-yin* 'Goddess of Compassion' (the Sanskrit Avalokitésvara) figures with their full, fleshy bodies seated in the *maharaja-lila* or position of royal ease (*plate* 131). The translation from a male to a female divinity is now complete. The ideal of the saint who

133 'Travelling Among the Mountains and Streams' in ink on silk by Fan Kuan (active 990-1020). This towering work is one of the most famous surviving in the early Chinese landscape style, Five Dynasties to Northern Sung period, (see also plate 118). This approach, modified in the Yüan dynasty, became the model for later artists of the scholar painter school (cf plate 218) who interpreted it on a more personal level.

Their theories of a fundamental harmony which existed in nature, a concept familiar from Taoism, stressed the indivisible unity of man and nature and the proper balance which should exist between them.

In the works of Fan Kuan, for example, we see man in his proper place and stature. He has painted the picture with minute care and due regard for the visual truth of his northern landscape. It is austere and infused with the dramatic vigour and spirituality which one expects of the tenth-eleventh centuries in China. Despite its meticulous drawing, the whole impression is one of inspired spontaneity, of the personal power of creation within the artist which matches

145

that of nature itself. Above all it is completely free of self-conscious technique and even more of sentimentality – the twin banes of later painters.

During the Sung period Imperial patronage of the arts was established on a magnificent level and produced some exquisite works, especially in the field of flower and bird paintings. An academy had existed at court since at least T'ang times and many emperors both prided themselves on their own calligraphy and painting and had gone to great lengths (including extortion) to assemble fine collections by the famous artists of their own and earlier times. When Emperor Hui-tsung (reigned 1082-1135), the last ruler of the Northern Sung and himself a painter, came to the dragon throne he gathered round himself a galaxy of brilliant artists and set a pattern for refined sensibilities which was the model for subsequent rulers in both China and Japan. The products of his entourage had the profoundest influence on all the arts of the East. The birds and flowers of eighteenth century porcelain owe much to him and his academy.

The academy served both to support eminent artists and to train younger men. Examinations were held at which painters were required to illustrate themes such as 'The scent of trampled flowers follows the hoofs of the returning horse'. A painter was on duty nightly at the court in case his services might be required to record some notable event. The one flaw in this idyllic picture of generous royal patronage was that Hui-tsung considered himself an infallible arbiter of taste. Surrounded by sycophants both able and not so able, he had no hesitation in supressing works which did not agree with his personal standards. As a result many of the most original artists, especially those who worked in the spontaneous, abbreviated ink-styles rather than in the favoured naturalistic coloured mode, chose to practice outside the charmed circle. If the Emperor liked a picture he would often deign to put his own seal or signature upon it – a habit which has seriously hindered art historians seeking works genuinely originating from his hand.

Plate 134 'Parakeet on the Branch of a Blossoming Tree', dated 1107, is a typical example of the kind of bird and flower painting for which Hui-tsung was famed. It is technically perfect both in

134 'Five-coloured Parakeet on the Branch of a Blossoming Apricot Tree' in ink and colour on silk, with calligraphy, attributed to Emperor Hui-tsung (1082-1135). Countless painters and ceramic decorators were influenced by such work, flourishing for the first time as a separate genre under the Sung.

colour and brush work, beautifully balanced and matched with a short inscription in Hui-tsung's fine firm, austere calligraphy. No knowledge of Chinese is necessary to appreciate the refined fastidiousness of the man from the drawing of the characters alone.

The pleasure loving atmosphere of this court was shattered by the invasion from the north. The Emperor himself was captured and died in captivity. Meanwhile the new Emperor and his court gathered the remains of their civilization and regrouped at the beautiful lake-surrounded city of Hang-chou there to continue what they could of their old life of art and sensibility. The beauties of the scenery acted as an inspiration and an escape from the somewhat sad atmosphere of the last century of a dying régime. Works of great delicacy in all the arts were produced which the rest of the East strove to emulate in the following centuries.

The southern Sung court produced many oustanding painters but without doubt the dominating style was that created by Ma Yüan and Hsia Kuei, cumulatively known as the Ma-Hsia School. Ma Yüan (active 1190-c 1240) came of a long family of painters. He was known as 'One Corner Ma' from his tendency to emphasize one corner of a landscape. A typical composition (*plate* 135) would show a figure under a gnarled tree gazing out over a chasm or a stretch of calm water into

135 Landscape in ink on a silk fan by Ma Yüan (active 1190-1230) of the Southern Sung Academy. This kind of romantic interpretation in which man is the emotional centre of the scene (contrast plates 118, 133) became the model for academic painters in Ming China and in Korea and Japan (plate 195).

an empty void.   A mountain generally soars in the background shrouded in mist.   Instead of the calm and detached observation of awesome landscape such as we saw in the tenth century, man and his reaction to nature has become the key.   The empty evocative spaces become the focal points of these lyrical landscapes which in the hand of masters are of great charm.   As Siren says 'The artist suggests infinity not only by utilizing empty space as a potent factor in the composition, but also as a reflection in the soul of man'.   In fact man has become the centre of the artist's interest and landscape is a backdrop against which he projects his emotions.   Such visions became highly popular in Japan and via Japan influenced the Western idea of Chinese painting. In the hands of later imitators, the genre is dangerously near to sentimentality and downright whimsy.

148

136 Hsia Kuei (active 1180-1230) is renowned for his axe-like brushstrokes. The landscape scroll, of which this is a part, is read horizontally section by section, unrolling changes in scene and mood, adding the time element to painting (cf plate 118). The form and Hsia Kuei's style were both taken up in Japan (plate 189).

Hsia Kuei, the other outstanding painter of the school served the court during the period 1195-1224 but much less is known of him and his background. His style as shown in *plate 136* is bolder and less sentimental than that of Ma Yüan. The ink tones for which he was famous have a rich luminosity. He seems to dissect nature rather than select from it and at times his 'axe-like' brush strokes are almost violent in their abbreviation. The speed and mastery of the execution give his landscapes a restless, time swept atmosphere. The deceptive simplicity of their style trapped many Chinese and Japanese into facile imitation. In his long handscrolls of which this is a detail, the composition has been likened to a musical composition, 'a symphony of black and white', in which the spectator is carried through an ever changing panorama. Such scrolls with their ability to add the sense of time to landscape are one of the great achievements of Chinese painting and at the hands of such a virtuoso bring full appreciation of the subtlety, the skill, the chromatic possibilities of Chinese brush and ink. The Japanese were to exploit the form brilliantly (see *pp* 161-3). Julian Huxley in his *The Humanist Frame* says that 'The important ends of man's life include the creation and enjoyment of beauty, both natural and man-made... the preservation of all sources of pure wonder and delight, like fine scenery, wild animals in freedom, or unspoiled nature; the attainment of inner peace and harmony..' In all these. Sung Chinese must rate as one of the world's most civilized times and people.

Buddhism as a source of inspiration had been declining in the last years of the T'ang but a new movement of major importance in the arts was to revive it. This was the Ch'an (Japanese: Zen) system. Supposedly introduced into China at the beginning of the sixth century by the Indian missionary Bodhidharma, it eschews all intellectual processes in the progress towards individual enlightenment. Enlightenment comes to a man in a sudden flash. Books, theological argument, icons, all the normal aids to faith, are useless. An essential corollary to this was that Buddhahood, ultimate wisdom, reality, call it what you will, pervades every single aspect of nature. It is as evident in a grain of sand as in a saint. The doctrine did not fall on completely unprepared soil, for Taoism – equally anti-logical, anti-social, achieving everything by a positive course of non-action, seeking identification with the universe, as a means to supreme wisdom — had already prepared one side of the Chinese mind for its teachings. The nature of Ch'an Buddhism was such that it made an appeal to both intellectual and non-intellectual, and in a world where printing had raised the standards of literacy this was important.

This new vision of Buddhism had the most profound effect on the art of the Far East. The concept of sudden enlightenment applied to painting created a style of ink painting in which the artist executed his work with the utmost speed and economy of line. This suited the king of brushwork for which calligraphy had already provided a lengthy training. Secondly, and more important, it taught men to look for Buddhahood in every aspect of nature. Thus a withered twig or a fruit contained as much of the ultimate truth as the grandest scale

137 'Six Persimmons' in ink on paper by Mu Ch'i (active 1200-1255). A Ch'an, or Zen, still life of characteristically deceptive simplicity.

Buddhist composition. This profoundly new outlook widened and deepened the scope of painting. It resulted in some of the most moving and most vital painting the world has produced. The most unpretentious motifs suddenly acquired a deep spiritual value. Hsieh Ho's injunction to seek the life giving spirit now became to seek the spirit giving life in everything. A still life of fruit (*plate* 137), a sweeping branch of plum blossom, a few strokes of ink play – through them all runs a new enriching current of emotion.

151

Ch'an painters in this period made their greatest contribution to Chinese painting. Living outside the restrictions of the academies they felt free to follow their own inner compulsions and a need to try to express the reality which lay behind external appearances. To do this, to reach this truth, they needed to meditate, to achieve sudden enlightenment, to develop their intuitive faculty. For them, sense and intellect faded before the sudden realisation of the inherent oneness of all life. A love of nature and a rustic simplicity were often the outward forms of this long discipline. They liked to consider themselves *I-p'in* or 'untrammelled' and yet their works reveal a supreme technical skill. Although seemingly simple, they are in fact the outcome of long reflection. They often give the appearance of being very hastily executed but each stroke is imbued with life as vibrant and meaningful as the object it depicts. This was a mode which the Japanese took up with enthusiasm and which they continued long after it had withered in China. It is alive today.

In Korea the Koryō dynasty (918-1392) was founded half a century before the Sung and lasted just over a century after it collapsed. The weakness of the Sung and the fact that the northerners cut off communications with China (1113-1234) resulted in less political contact. Nevertheless the cultural appeal of China was just as strong, especially during the first two centuries of the Sung dynasty when it controlled the north. The capital of the Koryō at Kaesong was a splendid city laid out on Chinese lines, the country was governed by a T'ang style bureaucracy and the Koreans adopted the Chinese civil service examination system in order to recruit state officials but still restricted it to the aristocratic class. Class distinctions were always clearly drawn.

Buddhism was dominant in both high and low born and Ch'an (Zen) and T'ien-t'ai were the most popular sects. In quality of printing the Koreans were always ahead of the other Eastern countries. They printed the Buddhist scriptures so beautifully, and, through the invention of moveable type, were able to disseminate them so widely that in these respects even China could not compare.

A few religious paintings have survived from this period but it is for its pottery and porcelain that the Koryō period is justly renowned.

138, 139 Two lidded wine pots in celadon ware inspired by the Sung Chinese but unmistakably Korean — one with incised and raised bamboo and leaf design, the other inlaid with delicate designs of lotus and chrysanthemum blossoms. Eleventh-twelfth century Koryō dynasty.

At their finest they rival the best that Sung China could produce and are among the ceramic masterpieces of the world.

The famous Korean celadons owe their inspiration to the Yüch wares (*plate* 117) of Chekiang province and Chinese potters may even have taught them. Towards the end of the tenth century they were producing crude celadons and within a century they had mastered the technique required to produce perfect wares. Even the Chinese were impressed by the Korean 'kingfisher colour' porcelains (*plate* 138).

In the twelfth century the Koreans invented the technique of in-laying different coloured clays to produce black and white decorations on their celadon wares, a type of ware which is unique to Korea (*plate* 142) and which has produced some of the most striking vessels to have come out of the East. Korean art has been called a 'lonely

153

art'. It has indeed a calm detachment, a quiet sense of isolation which distinguishes it. The shapes too are often quite different from those of China. As, for example, are the baluster shaped vases with very slender drawn-in bodies and exaggerated shoulders. Yet another type is the painted celadon decorated in white or black under the glaze in styles strongly influenced by the Chinese wares of Tz'u-chou (*plate* 141). By the beginning of the thirteenth century the difficult techniques by which celadons had been produced seem to have been forgotten. Instead of a reducing kiln the potters began to use an oxidizing kiln and the result was brownish or yellowish wares which are coarse by comparison with the earlier wares. Nevertheless, the Korean gift for lively decoration persists.

The Koreans took much from China but they preserved a high degree of independence in the shapes they created. This is illustrated by one of the most beautiful objects in gold and silver which has come out of the Far East. The ewer in *plate* 140 has porcelain counterparts and must have been inspired by Chinese T'ang workmanship – though nothing comparable has survived from China. The elegance and fine workmanship give witness to the taste and skill of Koryō silversmiths which match the quality of Koryō porcelain.

In Japan in the mid-twelfth century momentous changes were taking place. The power of the Fujiwara passed into the hands of provincial landowners some of whom were almost independent and were hard pressed by a militant church. The final struggle for power was won by the Minamoto clan who in 1185 established the Kamakura dictatorship which lasted until 1392. They established their headquarters at Kamakura, three hundred miles east of Kyoto, in an effort to preserve the vigour of the warriors from being sapped by the decadence of the capital. The elegance and refiniment of the preceeding period were frowned upon as weakness.

The Emperor and his nobles remained poor and powerless in Kyoto, their main function being to ratify the edicts of Kamakura. This was to remain the pattern until the restoration of the monarchy in 1868. It was the age of the samurai, of the worship of the sword and of duty, of valiant deeds such as the repulsion of the two large scale Mongol invasions of 1274 and 1281.

140 An exquisite Korean silver
ewer with gold decorations, eleventh-twelfth century Koryō dynasty. Nothing comparable has
survived from China.

141 Large Korean vase for plum
blossom, of celadon painted in
iron oxide under the glaze. Directly inspired by the Chinese Sung
dynasty Tz'u-chou ware. (plate
123)

142 Large Korean water bowl
with lion-headed handles with
inlaid black and white clay design
of a peony. Twelfth century,
Koryō dynasty. This type of
celadon is unique to Korea.

143 144 Figure of a Buddhist monk from the newly rediscovered west Chinese cave-temples site of Mai-chi-shan. Eleventh-twelfth century. Such figures must have influenced Japanese sculptors of figures like the one opposite, a portrait of the priest Mūchaku by Unkei (1142-1212) and his followers. A Japanese early thirteenth century coloured wood masterpiece of naturalistic sculpture.

During the wars leading up to the Kamakura régime much damage had been done to the old temples and their treasures. Now restoration work at Nara led many sculptors to revive straightforward ancient styles, but this Kamakura renaissance of Nara took on a more human form, the figures being less idealised, less spiritual.

Two of the greatest Kamakura artists are the sculptors Kōkei and Unkei. In portraiture, Unkei (1142-1212) and his school produced some of the noblest works ever created, e.g. the Mūchaku in the Kōfuku-ji (*plate* 144). To find their parallel one must turn again to China where the Sung dynasty had created its own styles (*plate* 143), and with which Japan was once more in direct contact. Realism was the basis of their approach and this tendency was emphasised by the Pure Land Sect of Buddhism which required icons which would appeal to a new wider public – likenesses of outstanding priests were celebrated in figures of uncompromising naturalism.

Colouring the outlook of these warriors was an appreciation of beauty at once strong and refined which has left a deep mark on all subsequent Japanese taste. Its mainspring was Zen Buddhism newly introduced from China where it had gained such great popularity

145, 146, 147 Japanese
Kamakura period styles:
two strong, Zen-inspired
portraits and a softer,
popular Buddhist icon.
Left: a non-religious portrait in silk of the warrior
Shigemori in court dress
by Takanobu (1142-
1205). Right: icon on
silk of Amida Buddha
descending from para-
dise to fetch the souls of
the faithful, by an un-
known artist. Far right:
portrait in ink and colour
on paper of the priest
Myōe Shōnin (1173-
1232) meditating on an
inspirational but realistic
mountain side, attributed
to Jōnin (13th century)

in the Sung period. Zen with its frugality and discipline, its simplicity
and rejection of the intellect, appealed to a fighting man. It eschewed
all religious icons. A few notable non-religious portraits of great
Kamakura patrons in their court dress were produced which are
completely divorced from the Chinese stream.

A few notable portraits of priests have also survived – as remarkable for their observation of personality as for their rendering of
natural scenery. Other forms of popular Buddhism shared in the
Kamakura humanizing process and became almost sentimental. A
popular icon (*plate* 146) shows Amida descending from his paradise
to carry the souls of the departed back with him to eternal bliss.

148 Part of a Kamakura handscroll, one of six illustrating the founding of the
Kegon sect of Buddhism in Korea, probably by Jōnin. A nobleman's daughter,
in love with Gishō, throws herself into the sea and, as a dragon, bears his ship
to Korea where he founds the sect. (p 160)

During this period the Japanese developed what they call *Yamato-e* or Japanese Painting as opposed to *Kara-e* or Chinese Painting. *Yamato-e* denoted paintings dealing with essentially Japanese topics and inspired by Japanese sentiments. The style sprang from Chinese T'ang dynasty coloured painting but became completely Japanised. The class included landscapes and genre scenes but most important of all were *monogatari-e*, or paintings illustrating stories. These were *e-makimono*, or handscrolls, unrolled section by section from right to left. As a result the scroll became a dynamic form of telling a story as well as adding the time element to pictorial art. In the early scrolls the various scenes were isolated by sections of calligraphy which provided a commentary to the story. Later, the writing disappeared and the artists developed most ingenious pictorial means of carrying the spectator over the hiatus between one scene and the next – banks of cloud, slopes of hills, surging waves lead the spectator on. The development of Buddhism amongst the masses through such teachings as the Pure Land stimulated the demand for a type of religious painting with secular subjects or references. The spread of literacy gave a wider public to paintings with literary themes. As *Yamato-e* the landscapes in these scrolls naturally have a strong Japanese flavour rather than being the plain imitations of Chinese scenery of the earlier *Kara-e*. Gold and silver often give them an added decorative brilliance and many are highly formalised.

The draughtsmanship, observation and sense of humour in these scrolls is often of the very highest order and in them the Japanese developed a pictorial sense of human drama which the Chinese never discovered. Two of the finest of these scrolls were produced towards the end of the Fujiwara period: 'The History of Mount Shigi' and the 'Animal Scrolls'. In both, line and ink are used almost to the complete exclusion of colour. Dramatic interest is perfectly matched with fluid composition. Each detail is a masterly study in movement and emotion. As Dietrich Seckel says, 'They charmingly and faithfully mirror the life of their day, secular and religious, aristocratic and popular. They reflect the sensitivity of Japanese lyric and epic poetry – if also the martial clangour of stark political and military reality. But most of all they represent a peak of perfection in the technique of

149 Scene from the twelfth century scroll story of Mt. Shigi in ink and slight colour on paper. The granary of a rich but mean man is being carried off by magic through the air.

the pictorial narrative which was never again achieved anywhere in the world. Only the Japanese with their deft and imaginative gift of composition, managed to grasp and exploit the innermost essence and fullest potentialities of the narrative scroll-picture, an art form which welds the representation of passing events in space and time into a perfect unity'. The scrolls provide an opportunity to point out some of the basic differences between the Japanese and the Chinese

150 Part of the twelfth century 'Animal Scrolls' in ink on paper attributed to Toba Sōjō, possibly a satire of contemporary clergy.

151 Scene from 'Jigoku Sōshi' ('Hell Scroll') by an unknown Japanese artist depicting the Hell of Measures where swindlers measure fire in iron boxes. Twelfth-thirteenth century. (p 160)

artist when working most clearly in their own traditions. I wrote elsewhere of this difference, 'Whereas the Chinese painter was fascinated by the grandeur of inaccessible mountains in all their moods, the Japanese used broad sweeps of colour washes sometimes without outlines to show his gentler native landscape. His brush was softer and calmer, expressing a lyricism which the Japanese attribute to their milder climate. The Chinese painter was awed by the overwhelming grandeur of nature and hinted at the delights that the human soul will find by seeking identity with it; the Japanese

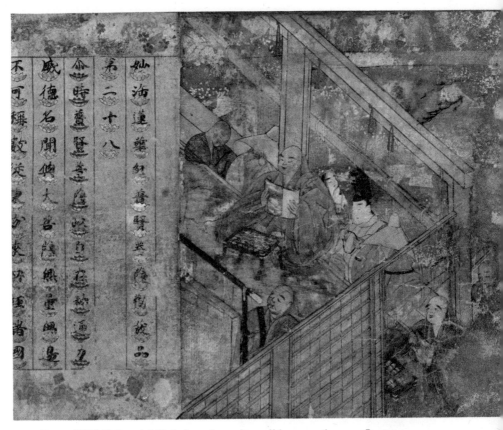

152 Part of 'Ichiji Rendai Hokekyō Sutra' scroll by an unknown Japanese artist of the late twelfth century, showing a gathering of nobles to read the Lotus Sutra.

approached his landscape in a more friendly mood and beckoned the spectator to share in its simple enjoyments. The spirit which in Chinese painting results from a deep mystical strain and produces the recluse has in Japan produced the flower-viewing parties which appeal to the native sense of form and colour. The instinct which led the Chinese artist respectfully to observe in a long landscape scroll the 'Thousand Miles of the Yangtze River' expresses itself at the hands of the Japanese painter in a more intimate view of the soft regular slopes of rolling hills'.

In the minor arts, the all pervading influence was again that of the Sung. Kilns were started at Seto, the great ceramic centre to be, and the potters strove to emulate the highly-fired brown and black wares of the Sung. The pieces which have survived have a rough masculinity, powerful shapes with vigorous freehand decoration.

In lacquer, Fujiwara styles persisted for some time. However, the most characteristic type of the time is known as *Kamakura-bori*, a type reputedly first made in T'ang China and of which a number of Ming examples have survived. Layer upon layer of lacquer is applied to build up a solid body of the material. This is then carved, generally in floral designs. The method was used for architectural decoration and sculptors are reported to have worked in the material.

153 Large vase with incized decoration from the Japanese Seto potteries. Early in their history, in the twelfth century, they produced such rough but vigorous emulations of Chinese Sung dynasty wares, especially *chien* and celadon then being imported in fairly large numbers.

CHAPTER SEVEN

China and Korea under Mongol domination

The Sung Dynasty had retreated from the Khitans in the north to found the Southern Sung. There they found themselves under pressure from the successors to the Khitans, a Tungusic people who took the Chinese name Chin, or 'Golden', Dynasty. The latter never achieved control of the Southern Sung and meanwhile to the north of them the Mongols were consolidating their power. In 1189 Jenghis Khan took over the leadership of these terrifying warriors. The Mongol campaigns of conquest which took them into Europe in the west, in the east swept away both Chin and Sung. The Chin retreated to Manchuria but were to reappear as the Manchu conquerors of China in the seventeenth century.

The invasion of China by the Mongols marked one of the periodic climaxes of the threat from the northern peoples. This time the conquest of China was complete. How an originally disorganized group of tribes could unite and, with less than two and a half million people at most, rise to such heights has never been properly explained. Extremely mobile, merciless fighters of great stamina, cunning tacticians, ruthless and dedicated to conquest and plunder they overran half the known world. Their harsh overlordship established peace across central Asia and their Pax Tartarica for the first time brought East and West into direct contact.

Kublai Khan (1215-94), the grandson of Jenghis, was responsible for overrunning China and establishing the Yüan dynasty (1260-1368). He had considerable difficulty in subduing the south of the country where his cavalry were of less value. Korea was completely conquered by 1258. Only the Japanese, with what seemed the divine aid of storms which scattered the Mongol fleet, and through the bravery of the Kamakura warriors, managed to resist the impact of the Mongol military machine. Japanese scrolls exist which show scenes from this valiant defence of the islands - they have been claimed as the first examples of pictorial war reporting.

The conquest of China presented the Mongols with a problem they could not solve. Basically this was the choice between whether to destroy China and turn it into a grazing ground for their flocks and horses or to enjoy its bounty and destroy themselves as a consequence. They vacillated and fortunately for China they chose the second alternative. They settled down to enjoy the benefits of a servile tax-paying community. Like other northern invaders before them, the Mongols found that they could administer the country only with the help of Chinese administrators and foreigners. The latter they welcomed and Marco Polo is, of course, the most famous of the Westerners who served at the Mongol court.

Though spiritually dead, the country was for a time ably administered while a flourishing internal and external trade brought a considerable degree of prosperity. However, the condition of the peasantry steadily deteriorated through constant forced labour, heavy taxation and the growth of tax-free lands. Economic conditions became so bad that as soon as a popular leader appeared with national rather than purely local ambitions, the country went over to him and the degenerate successors of Kublai were driven out of China with surprising ease. Chu Yüan-chang was the popular leader who achieved this and established the Ming dynasty in 1368.

Culturally, the period saw the flowering of popular drama – a medium through which the anonymous librettists could comment on their overlords and, because the Mongols came under its influence,

154 Deep saucer from Lungch'üan, the Sung Chinese kilns which continued production under the Mongol Yüan dynasty. This is the ideal celadon colour. (pp 138-140, 168)

155 Chinese Yüan dynasty dish of celadon glaze with raised decoration left unglazed in the biscuit, of a dragon chasing a flaming pearl surrounded by clouds. A popular allegory on later wares (plate 181). (p 168)

Tibetan Lamaism, a form of Buddhism which influenced architectural styles. In particular the Tibetan type of pagoda was popular in the fine Mongol capital at Khanbaliq (Peking).

Through international trade, a two-way cultural exchange took place. China gave the West via Persia painting and porcelain, textiles, gunpowder and paper money. From the West China took the religion of Islam, which the Mongols tolerated even after they had become converted to Lamaism, and which is still strong. Ideas from astronomy and music, influences from ceramic styles *inter alia,* were also felt in China. Persian metal shapes for example found their way into the repertoire of the Chinese potters. In return Chinese motifs such as the phoenix, dragon, lotus and peony and an increased naturalism strongly influenced the older Persian tradition of decoration.

The period of Mongol domination has often been dismissed as one of complete artistic destruction and intellectual sterility but this was certainly not so. We know nothing of mediaeval art in Mongolia but one of the few positive Mongol contributions to the arts of China seems to have been the introduction of carpet weaving in the north. However, nothing like a Mongol style can be postulated. Yet the

156 Large Chinese Yüan dynasty jar of Tz'u-chou ware with a band of glazed decoration on the shoulder against an unglazed background.

period was one of considerable intellectual ferment. The Pax Tartarica created a means of satisfying the great markets for Chinese porcelain in the Middle East. In this respect it must however be remembered that the famous northern kilns which had produced the *ting*, *ju*, Tz'u-chou and *kuan* wares of the northern Sung period had earlier been taken over by the Chin nomads and their great days were over. Only the *chün* and Tz'u-chou types continued to be made, coarser in technique and decorations. The Sung innovations in ceramics survived in the new kilns in the south, notably at Lung Ch'üan (*plate* 154) in Chekiang and at Ching-tê-chên in Kiangsi.

In ceramics John Ayers has summed up the Yüan period as ' marked by a strong change of emphasis in the forms, and in the introduction of various features of foreign inspirations; by a keen experimental interest in decorative techniques; and by a preference for elaborate naturalism in design so influential that it was eventually to culminate in a general triumph for painted ornament.'

To expand this a little – the shapes, particularly of celadons, became more heavy and less graceful than in the Sung. The decoration, often moulded and naturalistic, became heavy and sometimes downright clumsy by comparison with earlier norms. However, there are exceptions, as for example when raised designs, often of dragons, were left unglazed, their warm burnt red colour contrasting effectively with the green hue of the celadon (*plate* 155).

168

What is more important is that the Chekiang kilns had now a strong rival in those of Kiangsi, and from the early fourteenth century the ceramic centre of Ching-tê-chên steadily gained in importance. They first produced the *Shu-fu* wares – bowls and dishes expertly shaped and potted in hard white porcelain with a thick glaze only very slightly tinted with blue or green. Their decoration was of the moulded or slip type often including the two characters *shu* and *fu* meaning 'privy council' or 'central palace'. These wares form a bridge between the old *ting* and *ch'ing-pai* traditions and the blue-and-white which were henceforth to play such a large part in the history of Chinese ceramics. The *ch'ing-pai* glaze familiar from the Sung dynasty was sometimes employed for these new shapes but with an entirely new approach to decoration, one of the most notable features of which are designs made by applying threads of tiny pearls or beads (*plate* 158). Yet another notable introduction was in underglaze red painting on white porcelain – an innovation for which the Chinese may well be indebted to Korea for, according to some authorities, it was used there as early as the thirteenth century.

However, the most important departure of the period was without doubt the discovery in the early fourteenth century of painting in blue cobalt under the glaze, a revolutionary development which has

157, 158 Two Yüan dynasty innovations. Left: a bowl of the new *Shu-fu* wares with typical hard stoneware body and white with a faint touch of blue glaze. Right: a vase of the old *ch'ing-pai* ware but with pearl bead decoration characteristic of the Yüan period.

rightly been called one of the turning points in the history of Chinese ceramics. The improved trade routes across Central Asia facilitated the importation of cobalt, the Mohammedan blue, and the early pieces all seem to have used material coming from the west. The use of cobalt for over-glaze designs was common in the Near East as early as the ninth century and cobalt was used in T'ang dynasty wares (see *plate* 102). Under-glaze cobalt decoration seems to have been used first by Kashan potters in the thirteenth century on wares inspired by the Chinese Sung dynasty. However, the Chinese had better porcelain and their glazes united with the body far better than the Persian wares. They could also control the designs with greater accuracy. In the earliest pieces (*plate* 159) the blue is so dark as to be almost black and the decoration, though vigorous, is perhaps not up to the standard of the potting and glaze. However, the Chinese potters rapidly mastered the technique by the mid-fourteenth century and produced a blue decoration of splendid colour, resonance and assurance of design. The famous David vases dated 1351 show the speed with which the Chinese mastered the medium (*plate* 160).

159, 160, 161 More Yüan dynasty innovations. Left and middle: the revolutionary underglaze blue and white decoration. The large temple vase with elephant-head handles is dated 1351, a key to early blue and white wares. The simpler vase, in a Sung dynasty shape, is of the first half of the fourteenth century. Right: a handsome ewer with decoration in underglaze red, a type rarer than blue-and-white.

162, 163 Top: Flowers in the Sung dynasty style (plate 134) in colour on paper by the Chinese flower and insect painter Ch'ien Hsüan (c 1235-1297). Below: Two horses in colour on silk attributed to Chao Mêng-fu (active c 1226-1290).

The art which seems best to have survived Mongol domination was that of painting – a fact which testifies to the strength of the tradition. Many Chinese painters either refused to serve or were not allowed to serve the invaders but some found a place at court. Both Ch'ien Hsüan (c 1235-1297) in retirement and Chao Mêng-fu (active c 1226-1290) at Peking worked in the old Sung or even T'ang styles and the latter's horse paintings found particular favour with the horse-loving Mongols.

However, many of the loftier spirits preferred to retire and work in an atmosphere of political disengagement. Disillusioned with the

late Sung which had led China to what seemed the nadir of its des-
tinies, the literati returned for their inspiration to the masters of the
short period of the Five Dynasties and the great works of the early
Sung, to the tenth and eleventh centuries. They consciously rejected
the romanticism, the lyricism, the artificiality of the Southern Sung.
The 'Four Great Masters of the Yüan Period', Wu Chên (1280-1354),
Huang Kung-wang (1269-1354), Wang Mêng (c. 1309-1385) and Ni
Tsan (1301-1374) all worked at the end of the Mongol period when
conditions for artistic production were slightly better than at the
beginning of the period. They all aimed at a calm detachment, a
purity of spirit, a conscious underplaying of heroic features – in
other words a gentlemanly, scholarly objectivity in which they themselves seldom if ever intrude.

The technique of these typical literati painters saw important developments. In earlier times painters envisaged the final composition
from the beginning, and completed it without hesitation. Alterations
were not possible in the medium of brush and ink. However, during
the Sung period landscapists like Mi Fei had developed a technique
by which they could build up their forms by a series of dots and lines.
The Yüan painters carried this process to its logical conclusion and
henceforth, frequently discarded the use of outline and painstakingly
constructed their landscapes by a series of lines and strokes, dots and
hooks, often placed one upon the other. A composition could thus
develop with the artist's thoughts and could take a long period to
complete, sometimes as long as three years as was the case with
Huang Kung-wang's most famous landscape scroll (*plate* 165).

The effect of the Mongol invasions on Korea was perhaps more
devastating and more complete than it was on China. By the end of
the twelfth century the vitality of the Koryō was already at low ebb
and effective power had fallen into the hands of a succession of military adventurers. The Koreans had been under pressure since the
end of the tenth century from the Khitans of the Liao dynasty and
then from the Jürched who established the Chin dynasty. The Mongols in their turn invaded Korea in 1231 and rapidly brought the enfeebled country under their undisputed control. The Korean court tried to
resist by fleeing to a stronghold on an island off the west coast called

164, 165 Parts of landscape scrolls in ink on paper, by Wu Chên (1280-
1354) and Huang Kung-wang (1269-1354), two of the Four Great Masters
of the Yüan dynasty. Their detached view of nature (cf plate 133) and their
recluse spirits were greatly admired by later scholar painters.

Kanghwa and this so enraged the Mongols that they repeatedly
despoiled the land for the next two and a half centuries. When the
Kanghwa régime collapsed the country was completely ruled by the
Mongols and their princesses who were married to survivers of the
Koryō house. The two Mongol invasions of Japan further drained
Korea of men and supplies. To this were added Japanese piratical

attacks which devastated the richer coastal areas. When the Mongol régime in China collapsed the puppet Koryō régime in Korea rapidly disappeared, but the effect of the Mongol invasion and domination in Korea was such that we learn that by the end of this unhappy period they were able to produce in ceramics only rough, coarse wares with irregular shapes and discoloured glazes. The other arts seem to have suffered even more.

166 'The Jung Hsi Studio' in ink on paper by Ni Tsan (1301-1374), another of the Four Great Masters. This deceptively simple style —trees and empty hut in the foreground, stretch of water, foliage splashed mountains in the background — was considered to reflect a dispassionate nobility of character and was much imitated in later centuries. (p 232)

CHAPTER EIGHT

The Ming Dynasty: tradition and decoration

The downfall of the Mongols and the restoration of a native Chinese dynasty, the Ming (1368-1644), brought a sense of relief, self-respect and renewed purpose to the Chinese nation. During the previous four centuries all or part of the country had been under foreign control, so it naturally looked back for inspiration to the periods when China had been at its most powerful – particularly to the Han and T'ang. The weight of this venerable tradition weighed **very** heavily on the Ming painters.

Once the dynasty was firmly established the country began to enjoy peace and the prosperity it brought. The administration was efficiently organized. The educated classes developed ways of life, thought and art which were to survive until 1911. It was the great age of the collector and connoisseur. The Chinese aesthetic became fixed.

The stability which China now enjoyed contained the seeds of stagnation. Although Chinese armies for a while were once again dominant in Asia, culturally the Chinese were turned in upon themselves and ignored, often with disdain, the intellectual and political activities of the West. China developed a sense of cultural superiority which was not to be shattered until the nineteenth century.

The Ming dynasty achieved its early efficient administration through a vast bureaucracy which set increasing store on literacy and learning – hide-bound by tradition though they both were. Antiquarianism became almost a fetish. Confucianism achieved its greatest triumph and some of the emperors, their object being as much the love of

167 Detail from a typical Ming Chinese scholar-painter's scroll, ' Retired Scholars Among Waving Pines ' in ink on paper by Hsiang Shêng-mo (1597-1659).

learning as a desire to keep the scholars harmlessly occupied, launched vast projects of compilation. In the early years a new vitality, confidence and curiosity sent fleets across the Indian Ocean as far as the coast of Africa. However, the Chinese became increasingly concerned with the everlasting threat from the north and they soon lost the initiative in the sphere of foreign trade and expansion to Western countries like Portugal and Holland. An important development in Confucian thought was that of Wang Yang-ming (1472-1529) who carried one stage further the incorporation of Buddhist ideas into the native philosophy by stressing the importance of such Zen ideals as meditation and intuitive knowledge. These naturally influenced painting.

Painting under the Ming became essentially the preserve of the literati, the Confucian scholar-administrator class, and the wealthy land-owners who in cultural matters aped the scholars. The latter's ideal was retirement to a life of cultural pursuits for, although administrative service had its rewards, it also held its dangers – especially

176

in the second half of the dynasty. Jealous factions and distrustful eunuchs close to the Emperor gained sufficient power to scare men of virtue away from public service. Under the despotic system of the Ming emperors it was easy for corrupt politicians or court favourites to fabricate imagined wrongs which often brought summary and severe punishments to upright officials. Even a misconstrued poem or belle lettre or an imagined play on words could bring disaster. Painting, at least, was the most innocent of artistic activities.

Emperor Hsüan-tê (1426-35) tried to establish around himself a group of masters as had Hui-tsung in the Sung dynasty and he too both painted and aspired to act as an arbiter in the arts. Many accomplished bird and flower drawings were produced in the court but they were now generally large in scale to suit the flamboyant architecture of the age. The finest painter of his group was Tai Chin of the early fifteenth century who worked in a grandiose Southern Sung Academy style inspired by Ma Yüan. However, he soon threw off the restraints of court service and retired to follow his own artistic bent. His most famous scroll 'Fishermen on the River' (*plate* 168) is an intimate scene of life among the riverside dwellers and draws its inspiration from the Yüan dynasty recluses. Although Tai Chin died in poverty, later imitators of his style were numerous and he is credited with founding the Che School, so called from the first character of Chekiang, his birth place. The clear-cut vitality of his brushwork in particular influenced later painters, both in China and in Japan.

168 Part of the long Chinese scroll ' Fishermen on the River ' in ink on paper by Tai Chin (fifteenth century).

169 Landscape in ink on an album leaf by the most influential of Ming dynasty scholar painters, Shên Chou (1427-1509), founder of the Wu School in south China.

The other eminent school in the Ming dynasty was the Wu School which was centred on Suchou, the famous beauty spot and cultural centre of the south. Its founder and most outstanding master was Shên Chou (1427-1509) (*plate* 169). Despite his amateur, literati status, one feels that he would have found much in common with Tai Chin who was execrated for being a professional. Shên's successor, Wên Chêng-ming (1470-1559), the second great name in the school, was the apogee of the literati painter-scholar-poet – the complete cultured man. Chinese critics have never tired of equating his austerity and unwavering principles with the aloofness of his pictorial vision. In fact, his work, especially in his later years, shows a fine calligraphic vitality. From this time onwards the predominance of the literati was firmly established. Theorists like Mo Shih-lung and Tung Ch'i-ch'ang carefully fabricated historical background genealogical trees for this somewhat snobbistic attitude to painting which was to dominate the

170 Part of the Chinese scroll 'Seven Junipers', signed and dated 1532 by Wên Chêng-ming (1470-1559). An almost abstract painting of gnarled trees remarkable for its brushwork of bursting vitality.

following centuries. It became known as *Wen-jên-hua* or Literary men's painting. The theorists divided painting into Northern and Southern schools and the literati were supposed to follow the Southern school whose progenitor they claimed was Wang Wei of the T'ang (see *plate* 97). The so-called Southern School was said to have emphasised the use of ink rather than colour and strove for atmospheric effect. It is hardly necessary to point out that such distinctions were very often quite arbitrary and meaningless. Nevertheless they influenced the approach of many painters to their art and the Japanese followed the same general lines. *Wên-jên-hua* in Japanese becomes *Bun-gin-ga* and the Chinese *Nan Tsung Hua* or Southern School became the Japanese *Nan Ga*. It must be said that in later centuries the Japanese *Nan Ga* or *Bun-gin-ga* painters contributed more original works than the Chinese. This is certainly true of the nineteenth century.

Nevertheless, before the snob theorists really established the predominance of the amateur painter there was still great scope for the professional, even in Suchou the stronghold of the non-professionals. To tell the truth it is often extremely difficult to distinguish any difference in approach between the two streams of painting. Typical is the work of the two most eminent of the Ming 'professionals' T'ang Yin (1470-1523) and Ch'iu Ying (1510-1551) who were certainly literati by temperament and education but who lived by their paintings. The distinction between professional and non-professional is in fact an economic one and, although Chinese critics continued to apply it throughout later centuries, it is seldom valid. One can say of both T'ang Yin and Ch'iu Ying that they used colour more naturalistically, that they sometimes painted subjects such as

171 ' Poet and Two Courtesans ' in ink and colour on paper by T'ang Yin (1470-1523), one of the most eminent Chinese Ming professional painters. Such scenes, highly prized in his time, were scorned by the amateur scholar painters.

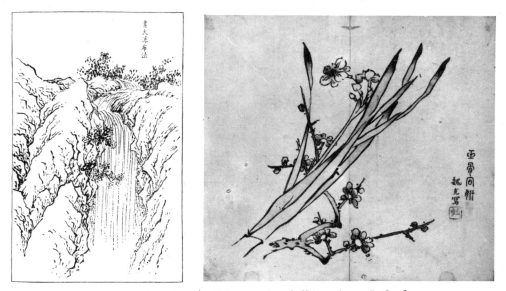

172, 173 Two examples of early Chinese printed illustrations. Left: from the 'Mustard Seed Garden' (1689 onwards). Right: from the 'Ten Bamboo Studio'. Compendiums of model compositions which, charming though they are, threatened to kill originality when used as stereotypes.

pretty women which appealed to the prospective buyer and that they both have suffered from later followers and imitators. Their works were repeated in the earliest wood-block prints, especially of erotic subjects culled from their somewhat purple lives in the pleasure quarters of Suchou. These in their turn stimulated the great wood-block print movement of Japan (see *plate 232*).

William Cohn pointed out the 'baroque' quality of Ming art – the pictorial method of vision and the unity of composition and space. Another baroque quality was the interest in the theory of painting. Towards the end of the Ming period there appeared compendiums such as *The Mustard Seed Garden* (1689 onwards) and *The Ten Bamboo Studio* (1st edition 1630)(*plates* 172, 173). These offered the tyro a complete range of types which he could copy and assemble at will to form felicitous compositions. Fascinating in themselves and often genuine works of art they carried within themselves the seeds of sterility.

174 Section of a Chinese handscroll of bamboos. Bamboo painting, a category in its own right, is closely allied to calligraphy. Here the painter, Hsü Wei (1521-1593), an 'individualist', is trying to break through the stifling formulae of other Ming painting.

To restore one's faith in the vitality of Chinese paintings we must turn to the work of a man like Hsü Wei (1521-1593) whose seemingly wild brushwork and careless calligraphy break noisily upon the studied calm of the literati painters. Only by violence it was felt could he and other painters like him purge the art. Such men were continuing a long line of artists who were philosophically inclined to Taoist meditation and Zen enlightenment, and whose private lives were as disorderly as those of the literati were ordered. Their work appeals strongly to one side of the Chinese temperament and its technique finds ready understanding in the modern West. It is the Chinese attempt to reassert the Hsieh Ho dictum which calls for a living spirit in art.

To turn to the other arts reveals more explicitly the character of Ming art. The tendency towards decoration seen in the Yüan blue-and-white became the dominant factor and varied methods of decoration were rapidly mastered. Whereas in earlier periods porcelain was made in many centres and was in the hands of local craftsmen, from Ming times onwards the industry was to be concentrated in a few large factories. The largest of these was at Ching-tê-chên in Kiangsi. Ideally situated to exploit the abundant local sources of raw material, a whole city grew up on this site devoted to porcelain manufacture. It was a porcelain of a hardness and whiteness not previously produced. As Lane says, 'The positive interest of the Ming porcelain lies in the outspoken contrast between the brilliant white material and the correspondingly brilliant coloured decoration applied to its surface'.

In blue-and-white, already by the late fourteenth century the whole surface of a vase could be covered with designs, generally of a pictorial nature. From then onwards and particularly in the Hsüan-tê period (1426-1435) the trend is towards refinement of body, glaze and drawing and towards repetitive designs in which chrysanthemums figure largely. The cobalt for the blue probably came from Persia, where it had been in use from the thirteenth century, and it produced varied hues from light blue to almost black. In places where the blue is concentrated almost to black the effect is what the Chinese call 'heaped and piled'. As the period progressed the

175 Chinese stem-bowl — a unique piece from the second half of the fourteenth century, early in the development of blue-and-white porcelain.

176 Ming dynasty Chinese bowl of blue-and-white porcelain from what is perhaps its finest period, both technically and artistically, the reign of Hsüan-tê (1426-1435)

Chinese learned to use their own less pure sources of cobalt and to produce with it a controlled uniform colour. Types were made with similar decoration in an attractive soft copper red but the material proved extremely difficult to control and it seems to have fallen from favour after about 1400. During the Chia Ching (1522-66) and Lung Ch'ing (1567-72) periods brilliant blue wares with a purplish tinge were produced and we learn that the annual orders from the Palace sometimes amounted to as much as 100,000 pieces. Of particular interest was the beginning of the export trade in the early sixteenth

177 Early Ming (1426-1435) Chinese porcelain dish with lightly incised white decoration on blue background.

178 Chinese Transitional Period (c 1620-1650) porcelain jar with a figure on a landscape background painted in blue.

179 Small Ming Chinese square dish with the mark of the Lung Ch'ing period (1567-1572).

180 Large Chinese jar of three-coloured Ming ware inspired by cloisonné metalwork.

century, first in the hands of the Portuguese, who established their Macao base in 1554, and later taken over by the Dutch. The trade during the reign of Emperor Wan-li (1573-1616) flooded Europe with technically inferior but lively blue-and-white wares. On some pieces the colours were effectively reserved.

The increased interest in landscape painting, probably encouraged by the painting manuals, found its expression on wares of the late Ming dynasty and what has recently become known as the Transitional Period (c. 1620-1650) between the Ming and the next dynasty, the Ch'ing. These have a fine quality paste with a slightly purplish blue like 'violets in milk' and show a new approach to porcelain decoration which was to be developed in the following century.

Of increasing importance to the industry from the beginning of the fifteenth century was imperial backing. Reign marks appear on vessels from the reign of Emperor Yung-lo (1403-1424) onwards. Many of them are a sure guide but in later periods it became the practice to put on an early mark out of respect for the achievements of a previous dynasty. In the nineteenth century these marks became little more than wishful thinking. Problems of dating do often arise in

181 A group of Chinese Ming mono-chrome and of enamel decorated wares showing the variety of colours and lively decoration of this period at its best. (p 188)

182 Chinese censer in cloisonné datable to the fifteenth century
by its decoration which resembles that on early blue-and-white
porcelain, in shape also reminiscent of archaic Chinese metalwork. (p 189)

183 Chinese late Ming dynasty *blanc-de-chine* porcelain figure of
Bodhidarma — founder of the Ch'an sect — crossing the Yangtze
river on a leaf, a development in baroque spirit on Sung dynasty
religious sculpture. (p 188)

184 Ming ivory figure of a seated official. It, like the porcelain
figure, has the keen sense of character that the Chinese used more
frequently in small scale sculpture than in large. (p 191)

earlier pieces with false marks. Imperial patronage has been one of the most constant spurs to maintaining the highest quality in ceramic manufacture.

The Ming monochromes in a sense indicate a return to the Sung taste for pieces of single colours in which shape and colour are left to speak for themselves (*plate* 181). The palette was enlarged with brilliant red, yellow and turquoise glazes of soft depth which are unlike the more brittle hues of the later centuries. A new technique of lasting importance, developed to satisfy the prevailing demand for decoration, was polychrome enamel which started in the Ch'êng-hua period (1465-87) first with red, and then green, yellow and aubergine (*tou ts'ai*). Lithe dragons in green encircle shallow dishes of the purest white porcelain. In later times a proliferation of colours and drawing brought the whole range of the painter onto porcelain. Indeed it is this amalgamation of the arts of painter and potter which distinguishes the ceramics of the Ming period and later.

The same qualities can be seen in the ware which perhaps reflects the Ming artistic taste most closely – the *fa-hua*, 'cloisonné', or *san-ts'ai*, 'three-coloured' wares. On this heavy ware turquoise, purple and yellow glazes predominate. The designs are outlined or restricted by raised threads of clay. The bodies of the vessels are sometimes pierced into lattice-work designs which further break up the surface and create a sense of monumentality. The best of these wares have a rare felicity of colour and delicacy of drawing but at worst they can be most clumsy. There is little doubt that monumental pieces of this ware were developed to match the grandiose rebuilding of the imperial city. The Ming emperors were above all interested in impressive building and modern Peking owes much to their efforts.

One cannot leave Ming ceramics without considering a ware which combines the skills of the ceramic worker and the sculptor, the *tê-hua*, or *blanc-de-chine*, wares of Fukien province. The figures moulded in this dead, white or creamy-white ware with their graceful, flowing drapery were first produced in the Ming period (*plate* 183). Whereas most Ming sculpture is clumsy these elegant figures carry on from where the sculptors of the Sung dynasty finished. This has always been one of the few materials in which the Chinese explore the possibilities of character in face and figure.

One of the most interesting innovations of the Ming dynasty was the use of enamels on metalwork – a technique introduced from the west as its Chinese name *Fa-lan* (the Chinese word for Byzantium) suggests. In China enamelwork generally took the form of *cloisonné* and the earliest pieces date from the fifteenth century. They can be dated this early by the similarity of their decoration with that of the blue-and-white porcelain of the same period. The finest are said to have been made in the Ching-t'ai period (1450-1456).

To the Ming dynasty or at least the fourteenth century we owe the development of carved red lacquer which people generally think of as 'Chinese lacquer' (*plate* 185). The manufacture of these pieces is a

185 Chinese Ming dynasty cup and stand in red lacquer carved in a design of phoenixes on a peony scroll background, inscribed with a poem of 1781 but with a date mark 1403-1424.

189

186 Imperial Chinese table of red carved lacquer made in the Hsüan-tê period (1426-1435).

laborious process involving the application of coat after coat of the liquid until it is thick enough to carve. Sometimes different colours are used so that as the carver cuts through the layers he can reveal the different colours and incorporate them into the design. This and the next century's designs, generally flowers or landscapes with figures and buildings, have a bold simplicity and fill all the available space. The red is remarkable for its rich dark hue resembling sealing wax. In some pieces the lacquer is used like oil paints on wood (*plate* 187).

The Ming period is also notable for its fine furniture and although we know relatively little about the history of this art, pieces dating from the fifteenth and sixteenth centuries can be recognised. They have a simplicity of decoration, a lack of fussiness and distinctly bold proportions.

These same characteristics of simplicity and a respect for the natural beauty of a material which had always qualified Chinese art in the past give Ming carved ivory its unique quality (*plate* 184). In later times virtuosity of carving destroyed the art.

187 Rear view of an early fifteenth century Imperial Chinese cabinet in red and gold lacquer with painted design of phoenix and a dragon, Imperial emblems, on cloud scroll and floral background.

CHAPTER NINE

Japan and Korea c 1400-1600:
the Ashikaga Period and the beginning of the Yi Dynasty

While the Ming period lasted its three centuries (1368-1644), Japan saw the end of one régime (the Kamakura, 1185-1336, which we have already discussed) and two others come and go, the Ashikaga, sometimes known as the Muromachi Period (1338-1537) and the short Momoyama (1537-1616), short but so important to the future of Japanese art that it will need a separate chapter (chapter ten). In Korea the Yi dynasty was founded in 1392 and was to continue until 1910, making it the longest dynasty in Far Eastern history (see later).

The Japanese Kamakura rulers over the centuries lost their single-minded authority over the various semi-independent families and after a period of disputed succession (the Northern and Southern Courts Period, 1336-92), the seat of power returned once more to Kyoto. This time it was the Ashikaga family who as Shōguns, or Commanders-in-Chief, ruled the country behind a façade of Imperial restoration. The most notable of these *de facto* rulers were Yoshimitsu (1368-1408) and Yoshimasa (1449-1490) and both of these potentates were devoted to the arts.

Once back in Kyoto and free from the austerities of Kamakura the court turned to a life of luxury. To satisfy it trade with China grew rapidly and part of this trade was in Chinese works of art, particularly paintings for the Shōgun's collections, which were to serve as models for Japanese painters. A virile merchant class also emerged which expected to be able to buy those artistic embellishments which the nobility acquired as if by right. The emergence of patrons of the arts among the merchant classes happened much

188 Landscape in ink on paper by Shūbun (active first half of the fifteenth century). A Japanese scholar painter's imaginary Chinese landscape inspired by Northern Sung and Yüan styles as reinterpreted by Ming Chinese painters (cf plates 118,165). (p 194)

earlier in Japan than in China and by giving artists security and independence produced an atmosphere in Japan akin to that of modern times in the West.

The local feudal courts also welcomed men of letters and artists for the cultural cachet they imparted. Beautiful temples were built, gems of preciosity placed in delightful natural settings (*plate* 190). There retired dictators could amuse themselves with the arts while at the same time manipulating the strings of power. Yoshimasa prided himself on his collection of Chinese paintings which included many Southern Sung landscapes. Except in architecture, Japan was once more completely in the thrall of China.

The influence of Zen Buddhism was still all important, though it was a Zen now coloured by the sophisticated outlook of Kyoto, and in painting China was again the source of inspiration. Zen ink styles became popular from the mid-fourteenth century, displacing the more colourful *Yamato-e*. In one field the Japanese seem to have surpassed the Chinese, namely in portraiture and figure painting. Odd amusing figures like Hotei, the fat, smiling god, and Kanzan and Jittoku, the two seemingly simple priests, appealed particularly to the Japanese sense of humour. It also became the custom to make Zen portraits of great priests.

It is extremely difficult to divide the Japanese painters into schools at this time. Whether they were priests or laymen, professionals or amateurs, inside or outside the court, they all seem to have been quite eclectic in their sources of inspiration, drawing upon one or other of the great Chinese painters as they became known in Japan. The landscape masters of the Ashikaga 'Court Painting Bureau' such as the priest painter Shūbun (first half of fifteenth century), were inspired by Northern Sung and Yüan landscapes while at the same time being stimulated by what they could study in the Ashikaga Shōguns' collections. They painted highly idealized visions of what they imagined was the landscape of China. As one might expect, artificiality and mannerism rapidly crept in.

It is often a most difficult exercise to distinguish between Japanese and Chinese workmanship in the landscapes of early fifteenth century painters such as Shūbun and his followers, but where a good

189 Winter landscape by Sesshū (1420-1506) one of the first Japanese to apply Chinese styles (e. g. Hsia Kuei's) to native landscapes. (see also plate 190)

190 'Amano-Hashidate' in ink and slight colour on paper by Sesshū
(1420-1506). A beauty spot in Japan painted in an individual fusion of
Japanese and Yüan dynasty Chinese styles ideally suited to the gentler
Japanese scenery.

Chinese work relies on genuine inspiration from nature, the Japanese
tends to rely on brushwork, on the conventions and formulae built
up over the years. Japanese brushwork tends to be more angular,
more nervous, less fluid than the Chinese. But a sense of tame,
comfortable intimacy takes the place of the awe which inspired the
Chinese Yüan painters.

It is not fair, however, to dismiss Japanese ink painters in the Chinese style without dwelling upon a few very notable exceptions.
Sesshū (1420-1506), most famous of the fifteenth century masters,
would have been outstanding anywhere and indeed he greatly impressed the Chinese when he visited a monastery on the mainland.
He knew Chinese landscape at first hand. In his landscapes (*plate* 189)

191 Small seascape in ink on paper by the Japanese artist Sesson (1504-1589), an eminent successor of Sesshū in Chinese ink styles. The brush strokes are as outstandingly vital as were Hsia Kuei's in China (plate 136).

the ink is most intense and the brushwork so nervous and powerful that it borders on the violent. He could work in many styles but at his most individual he was an artist with a unique style who reinvigorated Chinese ink styles at a time when they were in the doldrums in China itself. He was ever prepared to rise above the snobbism which made Japanese ignore their own beautiful scenery in favour of an imaginary China. His paintings of the softer landscape of Japan are masterly. Sesshū's work stands comparison with anything produced in China and he had a number of eminent successors of whom the most outstanding was Sesson (1504-89).

In the same century another line of painters was formed through Nōami (1397-1494) a court painter, followed by Geiami (1431-85)

192 Waterfall in ink and colour washes on paper by Kanō Motonobu (1475-1550), one of the founders of a long line of Japanese court painters notable mainly for their somewhat stylized and often didactic but highly decorative works.

and Sōami, who died in 1525. In their work the Japanese tendency to simplify and seek the decorative, to stress rhythms and patterns, becomes increasingly marked. The same tendency is even more evident in the work of the painters of the Kanō School which was to reach its heights in the Momoyama and Tokugawa Periods (see chapters ten and twelve). This school of professional court painters started with Kanō Masanobu (c. 1434-1530) and Kanō Motonobu (1475-1550) and continued unbroken into the nineteenth century. Certainly the family contributed a very great deal to the arts of Japan. Opinions are very divided on their merits. They usually decorated large areas such as screens or doors with confident brush-work but with little pretension of genuine sentiments or reference to nature. As decoration, which is perhaps all they aspired to, they are masterly. However, they are not comparable with the Chinese landscapes, their distant inspiration.

It was unfortunate that the cult of the Chinese enabled so gifted a family as the Kanō painters to efface the native decorative style.

193 Landscape in ink on paper, one of a pair of screens by Sōami (died 1525). Here the Japanese tendency in Chinese style towards mannerism is marked.

This was, however, kept alive by another great family of painters, the Tosa. It originated in the early fifteenth century and occasionally enjoyed court favour. The old *Yamato-e* styles so productive during the Kamakura period were now largely in eclipse, and it was left to the Tosa native style painters to keep alive the Japanese love of brilliance and decoration and their gifts for genre painting. Colourful, intimate, witty and unaffected they reacted against the stiff Chinese modes of the Kanō and testify to the strength of the Japanese tradition. Their work was of particular importance for the development of Japanese arts and craft and for the emergence of the later colour print movement.

In ceramics the Japanese were equally under the influence of the Sung, but they had not the taste, traditions nor technical skills of the Chinese. Nor had they yet discovered the raw materials with which the objects of unsurpassed beauty which appeared during the Sung period were made. But the foundations of what was to become a great craft were laid at a number of manufacturing centres such as Tokoname, Shigaraki, Tama, Bizen, Echizen and Seto. Examples of all these manufactures have survived but from the first five of these 'Six Old Kilns of Japan' the wares are very rough and the admiration lavished on them is little more than the relatively modern and sophisticated Japanese fashion for rough craftwork. From Seto, however, came highly-fired jars and vases with black, green and yellow glazes. They are often incised with lively designs which stand out where the glaze is thick. The shapes and decoration are inspired by Sung examples probably brought back by Zen adepts – especially tea bowls of *chien* ware (*plate* 194). Considering the heights reached by the other crafts, the achievements in clay were disappointing.

Of far reaching significance for the craft in Japan was the stimulus for rustic wares which the tea ceremony provided. This was introduced from China in a simple form as practised on the mainland by Ch'an monks and developed and perfected in Japan by masters like Sen-no-Rikyū (1520-1591). Rough, misshapen wares (see *plate* 201) became very popular to offset the elegant, perfect Chinese porcelain. Every building had at least one room with a *toko-no-ma* or alcove which held a painting or a vase and acted as a spiritual focal point to the whole room. It is difficult to over-estimate the influence of the tea ceremony on the crafts from the comparisons it stimulated between elegance and rusticity, the insistence on quiet good taste and the search it encouraged for beauty in all things. For instance, it raised the simple iron tea-kettle to a lofty art form. The loving care which craftsmen used to place their designs on humble iron acted as a foil for richer materials, and these juxtapositions are still one of the prime motivators of Japanese taste. The whole ceremony was imbued with the Zen ideals of beauty to be found in the humblest objects, and of the satisfaction to be had from the quiet appreciation of a work of art.

194 A Chinese bowl in dark tortoiseshell glaze of the Sung dynasty *chien* ware (see also plate 126), which was very popular in Ashikaga Japan and was emulated by the Seto kilns, later to be so productive.

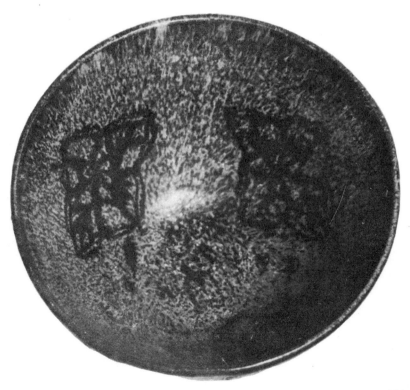

In Korea, although the Koryō had become a Mongol puppet régime, when the Mongols were defeated in China, the Korean rulers mistakenly threw in their lot with the exiled Mongols. General Yi Song-gye disagreed with this policy and with his army seized the capital in 1388. He assumed the throne in 1392 and established the Yi dynasty which was to survive until 1910. For those five centuries Korea was to become a cultural colony of China, its administration directed along the most rigid Confucian lines. The Chinese style scholar-administrator became the pattern for those who wished to enter the civil service but, as usual in Korea and Japan, with the important difference that the examinations were open only to the land-owner-official classes. In these examinations the Chu Hsi interpretation of the Confucian classics was exclusive. Thus a foreign culture reactionary in its country of origin and transmitted to Korea in a foreign language became all powerful and ultra-conservative. Buddhism fell completely from favour and ceased to provide any intellectual or religious stimulus.

The all powerful influence of China affected the arts of Korea very strongly. In painting, as in China, there was a conflict between professional and amateur. The scholar-administrators turned to painting on an essentially amateur basis just as the *wên-jên* did in China and, like the Japanese painters in the Chinese style, they were eclectic in their sources of inspiration. The 'Sage in Meditation' by Kang Hui-an (1419-65) looks like a typical Ming style interpretation of a Southern Sung theme, but it has a sense of humour which is Korean rather than Chinese. The brushwork shows the exaggerated strength which one associates with Japanese work. Portraits too were most skilfully executed – mostly by professional 'court' painters.

Korean authorities divide the Yi dynasty ceramic wares into two periods, separated by the Japanese invasion of 1592-8. Thus the first period falls conveniently into this chapter. The fine Koryō celadons of the previous period, since the Government owned kilns no longer operated, degenerated into a rustic, rough type known as *pun ch'ong* 'pale blue or green' ware. Its manufacture is coarse and often there is a coat of white slip brushed on freely, a technique known in Japan as *hakeme*. Some pieces have an all-over design of

195 'Sage in Meditation' in ink on a paper album leaf by the Korean painter Kang Hui-an (1419-1465). The style of Chinese painters like Ma Yüan transmuted by Ming painters are here given a Korean deftness and humour.

196 Jar of early Korean blue-and-white ware, a technique learned from Ming China in the early fifteenth century, decorated in a typically spare and impressionistic Korean manner.

tiny flowers filled with white slip, known in Japan as *mishima*. Occasionally bolder designs are filled with white or black slip. The Japanese names are important because these rough wares greatly influenced Japanese pottery after the Japanese invasion (see later). The imperfections in these hastily made, rough wares are compensated for by the very lively character of the designs.

A heavy white ware was also made but the influence of Ming blue-and-white rapidly made itself felt from the early fifteenth century. As in China the necessary cobalt had at first to be imported until by

1464 native sources had been found and the means of using them developed. It has been suggested that the characteristic sparse Korean decoration on these wares was due to the expense of the ore. The effect is singularly attractive.

In discussing the innate artistry of peasant-potters, Gompertz remarks that they 'worked with complete freedom to express their own concept of beauty, often in conditions of great hardship and poverty. The vessels they made were all strictly utilitarian; the material was rough and the potting often crude; but the forms and decoration – mostly painted in iron-brown or executed in sgraffito style on a ground of brushed white slip – possess a wild, free beauty that can hardly be equalled'. In blue-and-white 'The simplicity of the designs, mostly of birds and flowers, and the soft tone of the blue decoration combine to express a dreamy, poetic sensibility, which is as far removed from the elaborate Chinese blue-and-white designs as it is from the earlier Yi period brushwork in iron-brown or copper-red'.

The Japanese invaded Korea in 1592 and 1597 and took some of the potters back to Japan to stimulate their own ceramic industry in the south island of Kyūshū and there they strongly influenced the subsequent development of Japanese tea ceremony wares.

CHAPTER TEN

The Momoyama Period: Japanese taste

The Momoyama Period lasted only a few decades (1578-1615) but it merits a chapter to itself. A period of intense warfare, it laid the foundations of modern Japan and modern Japanese art. Both in colour and originality, its products were among the most brilliant which Japan has produced. Often and especially in the crafts they broke with the Chinese traditions which had long guided them. The whole output of the period is imbued with what is essentially a native Japanese love of decoration and a feeling for bold eccentric design which the Chinese never showed.

The founder of the new régime was a local lord, Oda Nobunaga, who, like so many dictators before him, had consolidated his strength in the provinces. He answered a call for help from the Emperor who repaid in the usual way by allowing Nobunaga to become the real power in the land. The new dictator was well served by his generals Toyotomi Hideyoshi and Tokugawa Ieyasu, men of humble origins who were destined to carry on his rule after his death by assassination in 1582. Historians make much of the fact that Hideyoshi was the first plebeian in Japanese history to rise to supreme power but it is difficult to see how this changed the pattern of Japanese political life or culture in any way.

It was Hideyoshi who launched the invasions of Korea in 1592 and 1597-8 partly with a view to keeping his military machine safely employed. During the second campaign Hideyoshi died and Tokugawa Ieyasu, after a long struggle for undisputed control, finally established his over-lordship in 1615. Thus began the long, peaceful

197 The Himeji Castle in Japan. The interiors of such structures, part palace, part fortification, were lightened and enhanced by the splendid screens of the Momoyama and Tokugawa periods. (see over)

isolated Tokugawa Period which lasted down to 1868. Artistically it is often extremely difficult to distinguish between the Momoyama and early Tokugawa periods. The division, an arbitrary one, can be justified only on grounds of expedience.

The Momoyama period takes its name from that of a castle which Hideyoshi built at Fushimi in 1593. Huge castles such as this one, part fortress, part palace, which combine architectural elegance and military strength in a most individual manner, were the Japanese answer to the introduction of firearms by the Portuguese in the mid-sixteenth century. The decorations which the Japanese devised to adorn them set the pattern for the arts of the period. The various provincial lords vied with each other to brighten their dim interiors

198 Plum trees by a riverside painted in ink and colour washes on a pair of sliding screens attributed to Kanō Eitoku (1534-1590), grandson of Kanō Motonobu and the most sought after painter to decorate the

with the most lavish products of the decorative arts. Huge screens and sliding doors combine the powerful outline ink painting of China with the colour of the native styles. Often these life-size paintings had gold or silver backgrounds to catch up and reflect the least glimmer of light.

The intention may well have been partly practical but certainly the new robust spirit suited the bold spirits who now guided Japan. The baroque spirit never produced more exciting works of art. The country was prosperous, the refinement of Kyoto, the simplicity of Kamakura, the Ashikaga respect for a China now in the last fading years of the Ming dynasty meant little to this new coarser generation of rulers who enjoyed their wealth and were determined that their minions should be impressed by it. The *recherché* Ashikaga atmosphere of tiny tea hut and rustic clay pot gave way to vast gardens lined

castles of the Japanese Momoyama lords. He was renowned for the strength of his brushwork and the lavish proportions of his screens.

with painted screens in which on occasions hundreds sat down to drink tea from golden vessels. The discreet alcove which offered but a few evocative brush strokes in black and white surrendered to vistas of florid colour in magnificent sweeps intended to overwhelm the senses. From these years of brilliant design and invention springs the general conception of what is essentially Japanese in Japanese art.

This was the period in which the Kanō School, stemming in the fifteenth century (chapter nine), gained further ground, but within it was great variety ranging from black and white essays in the Sung and Yüan manner to confident combinations of Chinese black ink outlines with the full palette of the Tosa school. Gold and silver backgrounds further embellished these large compositions. Kanō Eitoku (1543-1590) was the spokesman of this age (*plate* 198). His confidence and verve comes as a shock after the cool restraint of

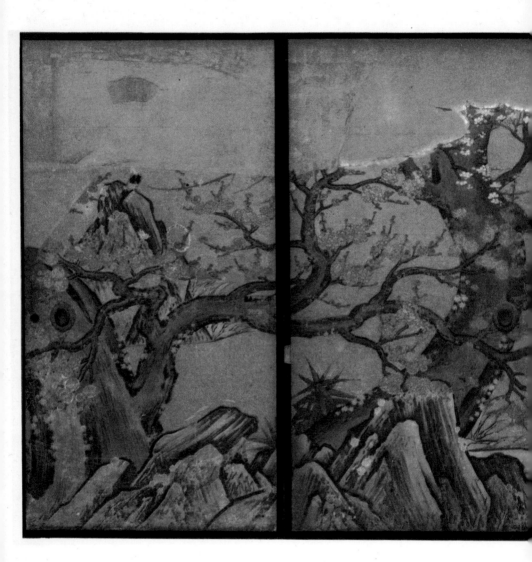

199 Four sliding doors of flowering plum trees in the style of
Kanō Sanraku (1559-1635). Sanraku, the adopted son of Eitoku (see
previous plate), worked in the great houses and temples of Kyoto.
This landscape against its gold background is typical of the
seventeenth century Kanō decorative school. On the back, the screens

have paintings of peonies. Originally in the Imperial Palace, they were later moved to the Daikaku-ji, Kyoto. The grandeur of this type of decoration influenced all subsequent Japanese art. Here, Chinese ink brush-work and the Japanese love of colour are brilliantly combined.

211

200 Pine forest, in ink on the paper of a pair of folding screens, by Hasegawa Tōhaku (1539-1610). It is the best example of an approach to screen
painting outside the colourful Kanō school, in which Chinese brush and

Ashikaga painting but in its ebullience and frank enjoyment of colour
one senses the joy of a new found freedom from Chinese influence.
If the Japanese are decorators *par excellence*, then their justification lies
in the art of this period.

While the Kanō School dominated the art world in the strongholds
of the feudal lords and at court, a few very notable artists worked
outside its ranks. Hasegawa Tōhaku (1539-1610) inherited the love
of Chinese monochrome but his approach to landscape is essentially
Japanese. He claimed artistic relationship to the great Sesshū and he
was one of the very few Japanese decorative artists who could inflate
the Chinese black and white style without destroying the delicacy
of the medium. His pine trees are dramatic without being
crude and are highly atmospheric in the best Chinese tradition
but the ink has a softness and modulation which are essentially
Japanese. The simplicity of the composition is both original and
moving.

As is to be expected, the tremendous impulse to decoration which
distinguished the art of the Momoyama Period, the love of colour and

ink are applied to great effect on a large scale but evoke in subtle monotone gradations and imaginative use of space a misty Japanese landscape in early morning.

pattern, had a strong influence on all the crafts. In ceramics many new kilns were founded in addition to those in the old established Seto area. The Seto potteries themselves were enriched by the Korean potters whom Hideyoshi brought back from his campaigns. The Shino wares of Seto – especially the Grey Shino (*plate* 203) - are distinguished by subtle designs executed with great freedom and vitality. Nothing is farther from the technical perfection of the Chinese wares. Both have their separate attraction and in recent times we have grown closer to the Japanese taste.

It is possible to mention only a few of the new products of this period. The Oribe wares, especially the decorated Oribe with their predominantly green glaze, have most original geometric designs of a modern flavour. Their thick glaze and conscious roughness of brushwork is typically Japanese. The shapes are often highly sculptured and show a constant search for what is new and unusual. Designs have a daring quality which is quite unlike the Chinese approach and which is strangely in harmony with Western art of three centuries later.

213

201 Early Japanese 'Raku' tea bowl of low-fired pottery with pinkish glaze made by Chōjiro (active 1576-1592). The dictator Hideyoshi gave Chōjiro's son a seal with the character for 'pleasure' ('raku') on it, and it has been the mark on the pottery his family have produced down to the present day.

In Kyoto a certain Chōjiro (1576-1592), originally a maker of roof tiles, began to make tea bowls – according to tradition under the guidance of that great arbiter of taste, the tea ceremony master, Sen-no-Rikyū. His 'Raku' low-fired pottery tea bowls with their black, white or pink glazes found immediate appreciation and fourteen generations of the family have continued to make such wares down to the present day. This type of bowl with its small foot, rough lustrous glaze and suggestion of fruit shape rapidly became the ideal of Japanese tea-ceremony ware – refined yet sturdy, useful yet beautiful in its quiet unassuming way. The Japanese potter seems to have been determined to stay close to the material of his medium, to reveal its intrusive qualities; the Chinese potter sought to transform it completely.

The sudden burst of brilliance and original design completely transformed the textile industry which under the Ashikaga régime had suffered badly. The flamboyance of the new rich demanded robes to match the brilliance of the screens and the extravagance of their entertainments. Thus the textile manufacturers were encouraged to explore every technique to the full – tie-dyeing, hand painting, embroidery, weaving, even gold foil *appliqué*! Different materials and decorative methods were combined in a manner which made the most of all possible contrasts. This was not a subtle art but one of breathtaking daring. The whole robe was often treated as a single decorative plane. This in itself is a basic feature of the Momoyama artistic approach. The result is a dramatic brilliance as effective as on the screens.

214

202 Japanese teapot of Oribe ware, so called after a late sixteenth century tea master who is supposed to have established the style, one that is exclusively Japanese in feeling. The decoration is geometric, and the bodies of much of this ware have a carved quality, quite un-Chinese. (p 213)

203 Momoyama Japanese square dish of Mouse-coloured Shino ware from the great Seto pottery centre. The ware's free-drawn grass designs recall Korean styles of decoration. (p 213)

204 Embroidered costume for the Noh theatre. Use of a single overriding motif, its boldness, and the startling contrasts are typical of Momoyama bravado in particular and since then of Japanese textiles in general. (p 214)

Seemingly incompatible features, colours and shapes, by sheer originality and bravado are made to harmonize. The textile workers laid the foundation for an industry which has never been surpassed.

The same originality is seen in the metalwork of the period. It was quite usual to inlay sword guards and fittings with gold and silver. The metal workers found new and closely guarded secret methods by which they could treat the alloys and common metals so that they took on new colours. The culmination of these techniques was undoubtedly in the following régime under which they will be discussed.

It is perhaps in lacquer that we see the Momoyama spirit and the Japanese sense of design most clearly expressed. It was highly sought after even in China, the home of lacquer. Unlike in the Ashikaga period when the tendency had been to decorate the surfaces with small neatly contained pictures, the lacquer workers now took a small segment or one feature of a design and splashed it gaily over the whole surface. Their ebullience often carried the designs beyond the borders of the pieces they decorated in a manner which stimulates the imagination. The craftsmen began the exploration of every aspect of nature which, for the next three centuries, brought a jewel-like beauty to even the smallest object.

The most characteristic type of Momoyama lacquer has the name Kōdai-ji, the name of a temple in Kyoto, to which Hideyoshi or his widow gave a number of pieces decorated in gold on black (*plate* 205). The boldness and simplicity, the dramatic contrasts and balance, control of colour and technique are the essence of Japanese design and are quite unlike anything produced in China.

205 Detail of a Japanese Momoyama period table top in Kōdai-ji lacquer with a design of autumn flowers in gold on black.

CHAPTER ELEVEN

The Ch'ing Dynasty, 1644-1911
The second half of the Yi Dynasty in Korea

The fall of the Ming followed patterns made familiar by former dynasties. Administrative corruption, eunuch venality, weak rulers and economic distress, allied to increasing external pressure from the north and now also from the Japanese, deprived the régime of the strength to resist disintegration. Popular uprisings within the country were followed by a full scale invasion by the Manchus, a Tungusic people from the north-east who had been learning Chinese style administrative organization beyond the Great Wall. A Chinese general stationed in the north asked the Manchus to assist him in putting down a rebellion led by a man who is said to have incensed him by stealing his favourite concubine. This general let the northerners through the Great Wall and thus gave the country over to nearly three centuries of foreign domination. It took the invaders some decades to subdue the more independent south, achieved only towards the end of the seventeenth century under the second Manchu emperor, K'ang-hsi (1662-1722). Under him and his successors, Yung-chêng (1723-25) and the long-lived Ch'ien-lung (1736-95), China fretted under a foreign yoke but enjoyed a period of great economic prosperity and political stability. The Manchus accepted Chinese culture but they, not altogether successfully, tried to preserve their national identity. They always remained somewhat on the defensive and were suspicious especially of the south. They tended to support conservative aspects of Chinese life and culture while many of the most independent spirits, finding themselves for one reason or another outside the administration, gathered in the ebullient intellectual areas of the south.

218

206 Large Chinese *famille verte* plate of the early Ch'ing dynasty K'ang-hsi period (1622-1722) in which the design shows how well brought-up ladies should occupy their spare time. Such pieces while showing high technical and artistic skill were produced in thousands at the porcelain city of Ching-tê-chên.

The Ch'ing Dynasty was a period of technical perfection in the decorative arts. In this respect Chinese porcelain reached its finest peak. After decline in the seventeenth century following the fall of the Ming and the rise of Ch'ing, the great factory at Ching-tê-chên in Kiangsi, backed by imperial patronage, produced a flood of superb porcelains, especially from 1693-1750. The blue-and-white of the eighteenth century, especially under K'ang-hsi, acquired a particular assurance of drawing and a brilliant resonance and depth of colour which are almost impossible to reproduce in print.

Allied to them the *famille verte* wares, decorated in green, yellow and aubergine enamels, incorporated the finest draughtsmanship with the most brilliant glazes. The *famille noire* type, which was basically *famille verte* colours on a black background, was one of the most treasured and expensive of porcelains. Later in the century, a rose

207, 208, 209 Ch'ing dynasty developments: technical refinement of body and variety of decoration. Top left: flamboyant and naturalistic flowers on a *famille noire* vase. Below left: rooster and flowers (cf plate 134) on a *famille rose* vase of *Ku-yüeh hsüan* ware. Below right: small vase in peach bloom glaze.

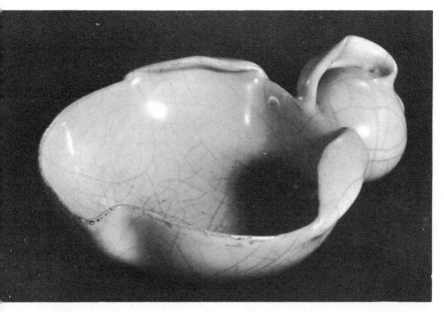

210 Chinese brush washer in the shape of a peach — an eighteenth century emulation of Sung dynasty *kuan* wares. It is sometimes only by the mark that one can distinguish them.

colour was added to the *famille verte* colours to produce what we know as *famille rose* wares. The cream of these is the delicate *Ku-yüeh hsüan* ware. The monochromes, through which many people first learn to love Chinese porcelain, were refined in technique but had lost something in subtlety of colour. The yellows and purples, in particular, became more brash than in the Ming, but, to compensate, many new colours were added – apple green, mirror black, *sang-de-boeuf*, *claire-de-lune*, peach bloom (*plate* 209) to mention only some. They have the precision and sparkle of gems.

The Ch'ing dynasty scholars were greatly interested in antique collecting and sponsored splendid reproductions of Sung dynasty wares, notably *kuan*. Were it not for the marks on the bases of some of these, they would be very difficult to distinguish from Sung wares. An interesting side-line was the export wares – especially the armorial

211 Chinese plate of the armorial porcelain for export to Europe, Africa, America and Russia. It bears the arms of the Clifford family, and is of the mid-eighteenth century.

porcelain. An eighteenth century gentleman in the West could take his book-plate to an East India Company representative, choose a design from a stock range and have a huge dinner service made in China at a fraction of what it would have cost him in Europe (*plate* 211).

The eighteenth century *blanc-de-chine* or *tê-hua* figures of Fukien province have a purity of white glaze allied to a finesse of modelling and a delicacy which made them the wonder of the West. Such porcelain, and especially the blue-and-white, was, of course, the inspiration of all European factories and one finds countless examples of Dutch, English and German copies of Chinese export wares. The range and quantity of production during this period are staggering. The European taste for tea and Chinese porcelain and Chinese disinterest in any foreign products resulted in a huge one-sided trade balance which the West could only redress by exporting opium.

212 Chinese *blanc-de-chine* figure of Kuan-yin, the Goddess of Compassion. The former male Bodhisattva at her most human, spirituality remains only in the abstractedness of her face. The purity of white glaze and daintiness of modelling in such figures were the inspiration of European Rococo potters.

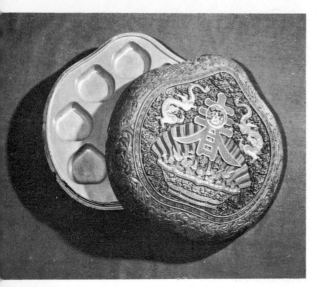

213 A Chinese Ch'ing dynasty
sweetmeat box of red, green and
yellow lacquer with the character
for 'spring' forming the central
motif.

214 Imperial Chinese throne in
red lacquer carved in dragons and
floral scrolls. A grandiose piece
which combines the boldness
characteristic of Ming dynasty
conceptions with the virtuosity
of Ch'ing carving.

215,216 Two examples of eighteenth century Chinese jade carving. The stylized landscape on the brushpot was a favourite Ch'ing theme.

The characteristic delicacy and intricate quality of Ch'ing workmanship shows at its best in the lacquer wares. Designs are more detailed than in the Ming period and the workmanship more clear cut. However, the Ming boldness, assurance and vigour were only too often lost in the minutiae and fussiness of these Ch'ing centuries. Decorations are often formal landscapes with tremendous detail on overworked floral designs. The colour is often less orange and more crude than in the Ming. The range of objects made from lacquer became larger – from tiny snuff bottles to huge furniture. A chair in the Victoria and Albert Museum is one of the largest and most impressive pieces of Ch'ing furniture to have found its way to the West.

Eighteenth century jadework is considered to be the finest ever produced. Since we know very little of Ming jade and have little that can be dated undisputably as Ming, we can make few valid comparisons. China's wealth in the eighteenth century and her taste for sumptuary art resulted in a tremendous demand for jade, not only from the Imperial house but also from the nobility and increasingly wealthy merchant classes. The emperors set up workshops within the Palace precincts in Peking and many others must also have existed. The jade itself came from all over the East and in colour ranged from pure white to the deepest of green. Examples of almost every other colour are found though one must not question too closely whether or not they are actually jade. Beautiful carvings were made in almost all the hardstones found in the East and here again archaism was very popular. Archaic vessels, brush pots, jade screens, huge boulders fashioned to represent mountain landscapes, hat stands, sceptres, massive official seals, animals of all types, bibelots of every description, poured from the workshops.

A tremendous amount of metalwork was made during the Ch'ing centuries. A considerable proportion was archaistic in approach, misunderstood inspirations of ancient bronzes of the Shang and Chou dynasties. It must be admitted that much of this is crude by comparison but it should be judged in an eighteenth century context, not as copies of work three thousand years old. As such it is much undervalued and it would repay study. The craftsmanship is often extremely fine. One of the types of metalwork which is popularly appreciated is known as Canton enamel. This painted enamel ware is done on copper in imitation of the *famille-rose* wares and was probably inspired by Limoges painted enamels. At its finest this Canton enamel has great attraction but much of it is rough by comparison with the porcelain it tries to emulate.

217 An eighteenth century gold inlaid version of an archaic bronze vessel. The decoration is a misunderstood simplification, but the standard of craftsmanship is high. The type is underrated.

218 Landscape by Wang Hui (1632-1717) in ink and colour on silk, that turns the towering mountains of Northern Sung and the severe detachement of Yüan landscapes into a classical invention in the style of an outstanding scholar/administrator painter. (p 228)

The tremendous expansion in all the arts and crafts of the Ch'ing dynasty was shared by painting. Many hundreds of painters are recorded in the official bibliographies and the standard of their work is on the whole remarkably high – though again it is often very much undervalued, especially by those who think that everything stopped with the Sung dynasty. The peace and prosperity of the country on the one hand produced a large class of civil servants for whom painting was an accepted leisure occupation, and on the other produced a class of wealthy patrons ready to support those unemployed intellectuals who lived by their calligraphy and painting.

Speaking in the broadest terms, the painters of the seventeenth and eighteenth centuries may be divided into two streams – the

219 Detail from a landscape scroll 'Spring Morning' by Wang Yüan-ch'i (1642-1715), another famous Ch'ing traditionalist. High viewpoint, lack of focal points, contribute to casual appreciation of a nevertheless skilful composition which incorporates nearly a thousand years' experience in landscape painting.

traditionalists and the individualists. Typical of the former were the so-called Six Great Masters of the Ch'ing Dynasty, namely the Four Wangs (Wang Shih-min 1592-1680, Wang Chien 1598-1677, Wang Hui 1632-1717, and Wang Yüan-ch'i 1642-1715) Wu Li (1632-1718) and Yün Shou-p'ing (1633-1690). They were all respectable scholarly men who followed the traditions of literary men's painting as formulated by their model Tung Ch'i-ch'ang. They aimed at being the complete cultured gentlemen equally adept as painter, calligrapher and poet. They were eclectic in approach, taking whatever appealed to them from the so-called Southern School and they greatly admired the works of the Sung and Yüan periods. All were virtuosi of the brush and their carefully organized landscapes are full of atmospheric detail. Many of their works are highly polished summaries of the vast experience in landscape which painting had by now built up. However, although pure in spirit and full of lofty ideals, they lack the power and sincerity of Yüan landscapes, for their sources were by now growing thoroughly hackneyed. Nothing, one feels, is being seen for the first time, no effort is made to suggest what might be new. An apt comparison might be the difference between the versifications of an eighteenth century English gentleman and the sonnets of Shakespeare. What they do reflect is a perfection of form and technique, a clear distillation of landscape as seen by a cultured Chinese scholar. Above all they have an intellectual purity which, like some of the Ch'ing ceramics, is almost gem-like.

Yün Shou-p'ing, who was outside the administration, ended by painting only flowers and insects and he also summarizes the experience of a long line of academy painters going back to the Northern Sung and even earlier. His work is sensitive and accurate without being botanical drawing in the dead sense of the word. Though classed as a *wên-jên* painter, he in fact lived by his art. He died a pauper and his funeral rites were paid for by his friend Wang Hui.

Yet, just as in nineteenth century Europe an equivalent of this type of painting stimulated a revolt, so a century or more earlier in China new forces were making themselves felt. The work of these 'fauves' is of greatly more importance in the history of Chinese painting than that of the mannered school for it signifies a determination to explore new avenues, to see the world with new eyes. Occasionally they become almost bizarre, but at their best the works of the individualists are among the finest of all Chinese paintings.

The earliest of these individualists was K'un Ts'an, also known as Shih-ch'i (active 1655-1675). He was a distant descendant of the Ming royal family and on the downfall of the dynasty became a Buddhist monk, even rising to the headship of a monastery. Unlike many painter-monks he took his religious duties seriously. He rejected the intellectualism of the past century and returned to the source of his inspiration which was nature itself. His soaring compositions owe much to the Yüan dynasty masters and he is less extravagant than many

220 Mountain landscape by K'un Ts'an (active 1655-1675), a famous Ch'ing
'individualist'. A real landscape and one which demands involvement, in contrast to the discreet, impersonal work of traditionalists.

221 'Kingfisher on a Lotus Stalk' by Chu Ta (c 1625-1700) in ink on paper.

later individualists. For him nature was a deep personal experience and his work reflects the calmness and humility of his spirit. It is humble but warm, his touch is delicate but his vision large enough to encompass the widest landscapes. The broad frame in which he organized his landscapes follow those of the Yüan masters but his technique summarizes the centuries following. He is individual only in so far as he rejects the intellectual in favour of the personal and emotional.

Chu Ta (c 1625-1700) is different. Better known as Pa-ta-shan-jên, he too was related to the Ming and retired from public life early in life. Dumbness ran in the family and he too was afflicted. Nevertheless, he kept up a lively correspondence with his friends, notably with Tao Chi (see later). His work falls into two fairly distinct categories, birds, flowers and fish etc. and landscapes. In the first his touch is unmistakeable. A few splashes of ink and a lonely fish gazes up at us from the depths of a pond, or a comic bird peers into the vastness of nature, a chick pecks a grain of food, or a spider in one corner waits ominously for its next meal. His humour is immediate and although countless tales are told of his wildness and excessive drinking habits, his paintings show a well-balanced human being. Chu Ta's landscapes are often much larger than his album leaves and many profess to admire Ni Tsan (see *plate* 166). One of the most fascinating aspects of Chinese painting is to follow the 'transformation' of past masters by later painters. This is a Far Eastern discipline consciously practised and not to be confused with empty copying.

In the chapter on the Ming dynasty we mentioned Hsü Wei (*page* 182) whose work breaks away from the *wên-jên* modes. A number of painters followed him in the Ch'ing period. The best known is Tao Chi (sometimes known as Shih-tao) who lived from 1630 to about 1714. Like K'un Ts'an he was related to the Ming royal family and found it expedient to retire to a Buddhist monastery where he devoted his life to painting. However, Buddhism seems to have sat lightly on his shoulders. His oft-quoted writings on painting have the same originality as his paintings. Although he admired the ancients, especially Ni Tsan, it was he who proclaimed that it was his ambition to 'transform' them, an ambition which was carried out by his friend Chu Ta as much as by him. His most famous saying is 'The beards and eyebrows of the ancient masters cannot grow on my face nor their lungs and bowels (thoughts and feelings) be transplanted into my stomach (spirit)'. This sums up an attitude which he expressed elsewhere as 'The method which consists of following no method is the best method'.

His work shows a conscious effort to break away from the rigid patterns which threatened to strangle Chinese painting. His landscapes differ from those of his contemporaries in that they are imbued with a genuine first-hand emotion. They are never well-worked formulae. Often they contain an element of humour which is equally valid in our civilization and time.

The individualist movement flourished while it could in such intellectual atmospheres as existed in southern cities like Hangchou and Yangchou, where wealthy merchants and civil servants supported unemployed artist scholars. Historians tend to group these

232

222 River landscape in ink and colour dated 1703 from an album by
Tao Chi, a Ch'ing individualist and famous theorist.

painters under the names of the cities where they gathered, which gives rise to names like The Eight Strange Masters of Yangchou or the Eight Masters of Nanking. The most notable of the latter was Kung Hsien (c 1617-1689). He painted in ink alone and with a starkness of tone which has caused Westerners to liken him to Altdorfer or El Greco. Modernists think of him as an·Eastern Van Gogh. His landscapes are almost violent in their power, nothing in them is artificial or mannered. Nature is not a playground or a vast garden, it is still mysterious and menacing.

The same individualist spirit often expressed itself in works of comparatively smaller scale, like albums where the calligraphy and painting are more closely integrated than before. A typical example is the work of Li Shan, one of the Eight Eccentrics of Yangchou. He is indebted to Hsü Wei and Pa-ta-shan-jên but is more sensitive than either of them. The ink and paper he used gives his tones a

223 Mountain landscape by Kung Hsien (c 1617-1689) in ink on paper, a work outside any traditional context. Jagged black-lined peaks which recede very little, cutting through thick clouds, without a skyline, create a two dimensional effect of ominous power.

224 Insects and calligraphy on an album leaf by Li Shan (first half of the eighteenth century) in the individualist ink styles started by men like Hsü Wei (plate 174).

new luminous quality. It is not difficult to see how indebted to him are the twentieth century painters like Ch'i Pai-shih.

The nineteenth century in Chinese art was a period of decline in artistic and technical standards. Initiative in the arts moved across the straits to Japan.

The second half of the Yi dynasty (c. 1590 onwards) opened badly for the Koreans. They first suffered from the Japanese invasion and then from the Chinese armies which came to Korea's aid and stayed to pillage. The scholar class who controlled the policies of the country made the further mistake of throwing Korea in on the side of the Ming against the rising power of the Manchus and this in its turn brought humiliation and hardship when the latter were triumphant. From their mistakes and trials, the conservative Confucian class emerged with their powers undiminished and their wisdom unenlarged. It was not until the eighteenth century that peace in China and Japanese isolation brought somewhat better conditions to Korea. Unlike the Chinese and Japanese, the Koreans seem to have welcomed Western innovations with enthusiasm.

225 'The Diamond Mountains' by Chong Son (1676-1759), a Korean hanging scroll of ink and colours on paper. The North Korean mountains famous for their needle peaks and the many Buddhist temples they shelter are here made even more fantastic.

It would be a mistake to read too much into the comparative independence which the Koreans won in that century but their painting certainly has qualities which distinguish it from both Chinese and Japanaese work. Some landscapes such as 'Diamond Mountains' by Chong Son (1676-1759) (*plate* 225) or 'Steep Heights' by Hong-do (1760- ?) (*plate* 227) have a conscious exaggeration which is distinct from Chinese conventions. Others, like 'Mountains and Rivers Without End' by Yi In-man (1746-1825) (*plate* 226) are frankly inspired by Ming examples but nevertheless they have a clarity and an interest in the minutiae of everyday life quite their own. The Koreans have a liking for fantastical landscapes which outdoes even the Chinese.

However, it is in genre painting that the Koreans made an individual contribution to Far Eastern painting. Typical is Sin Yun-bok's 'Boating Scene' (1758-1840) which incensed the Confucian moralists

226 Part of a handscroll of ink and faint colour on silk by Yi In-man (1746-1825), a Korean transformation of Sung/ Ming Chinese styles in which the influence of Hsia Kuei (plate 136) is noticeable.

227 'Steep Heights', an album leaf by the Korean painter Kim Hong-do (born 1760) who was strongly influenced by Chinese individualist painters like Tao Chi (plate 222).

228 A boating party genre scene on an album leaf by Sin Yun-bok (born 1758), typical of the wit Koreans brought to Far Eastern painting.

by showing men and women enjoying themselves together in what would appear to us as a harmless boating entertainment but to them as unashamed abandon. It has at the same time a *joie-de-vivre* and an unaffected dignity which makes one regret that the Koreans for only a relatively short time turned their hands to this type of painting. The Koreans, as their history amply illustrates, are an irrepressible people and in much of their painting there appears a calm and gentle sense of humour which the Chinese rarely show and which the Japanese may well have learned from them.

The pottery of the period shows a lapse from the high technical standards of previous centuries but this is compensated for by vigorous designs on energetic shapes. The underglaze iron red on a rough provincial food vessel in *plate* 229 is in the best pottercraftsman tradition even though the materials are somewhat coarse. Finer examples were also made in better quality materials but the most characteristic group were in underglaze blue (*plate* 230) where freehand painting, the work of sensitive craftsmen, is never automatic in its perfection as is the Chinese. It is not difficult to see whence the Japanese derived their sense of porcelain decoration.

229, 230 Eighteenth century Korean pots using techniques from China but in shape and decoration quite independent. Top: a jar of grey porcelain with decoration of vine leaves and tendrils under the grey in iron oxide. Below: a serving bowl in white porcelain with underglaze blue decoration.

CHAPTER TWELVE

Japan 1600-1868: The Tokugawa Period

When Nobunaga, founder of the Momoyama dictatorship, and his successor Hideyoshi, died, a struggle for power ensued. From this struggle, one of his generals, Tokugawa Ieyasu (1542-1616), emerged supreme in the islands. Nobunaga had enfeoffed this ambitious man of humble origins with the key central area of Japan. His strategic position gave him an opportunity to become the effective power in the land.

The régime he created governed Japan for over 250 years – roughly the same length of time as the Manchu dynasty governed China. It brought peace and great economic prosperity to the country.

However, unlike China which fell a prey to aggressive Western mercantilism, Japan recognised the threat from without, completely shut herself off from almost all physical contact with other nations and became to all intents and purposes a veritable hermit kingdom. This distrust of the West led, among other things, to a violent persecution of Christianity which the Japanese leaders saw as a cloak for imperialism. However, the isolation, though rigid, was never one hundred per cent effective. Cultural influences from both China and the West filtered through to the intellectually curious Japanese, mainly via the port of Nagasaki which remained partially open. Nevertheless, in most cultural and artistic matters Japan was turned in upon itself and in this hothouse atmosphere of isolation and prosperity produced some of its most individual works of art.

Both China and Japan experienced a rapid growth in population during the first centuries of the new régimes. A feature of Japanese social life at this time was the rapid growth of the urban population. The *daimyō*, the great local lords, were at first prosperous and artistic extravagance was for them one of the only ways of spending their money safely. The government, in good Confucian manner, paid lip-service to the farming classes but increasingly taxed them out of existence. Nothing seemed able to stop the merchants augmenting their power and wealth. On occasions the rulers tried to curb them, even to the extent of confiscating the fortunes of the most blatant, but the total effect was negligible. The merchants quite quickly took over the financial lead from the *daimyō*.

It was the urban population, the merchants and their employees in the big cities, who put the stamp on much of Japanese Tokugawa period life. In China a few merchants notably in the south gained wealth and cultural status but they tended to use their money in the support of traditional modes. They did support individualistic artists and re-negades from the civil service but they and their servants did not create or support an art of their own. The urban class in China hardly counted. The Japanese of cities like Edo (modern Tokyo) displayed a tremendous energy which very often seemed to find expression in artistic ways – even when the form was erotic, it was still highly artistic. They were completely confident of their strength and of the benefits which their wealth could bring them. They were sometimes bawdy in the Shakespearian sense but they had wit and in art they demanded very high standards. They expected their artists to be original and took for granted a standard of craftsmanship which has never been surpassed anywhere in the world. Their taste expressed itself in a mixture of richness and restraint, swaggering ebullience and delicate wistfulness. It was as if the tremendous forces which created the industrial revolution in the West were in Japan turned into artistic channels.

Perhaps the most extraordinary artistic phenomenon of the Tokugawa period was the colour-print movement, the *ukiyo-e*, or painting of the floating, fleeting world. The origins of the wood block printing technique can be traced back to China where in the T'ang dynasty Buddhist iconographical pictures were printed in black and white outline. In Japan during the Fujiwara centuries wood blocks were

240

231, 232 Japanese wood-block prints of two of the most popular themes of the print movement, an actor of the Kabuki theatre by Kunisada (1786-1864) one of the last great masters, and two courtesans by Utamaro (1754-1806), the master of the female figure.

used for decorative papers which formed backgrounds for Buddhist texts. In the late Ming period many book illustrators used the technique and we have already mentioned the famous instruction manuals for painting (see *plates* 172/3). Wood blocks were used in China during the late Ming quite extensively for erotic illustrations in which the main interest was hardly artistic and technical standards are low.

However, the skilful hands of the Japanese raised this art to supreme heights. It became an expression of the plebeian population of the cities – especially Edo, the seat of the Tokugawa Shōguns. This ebullient, witty population, the product of a changed cultural and social structure, demanded an art which was topical, lively and cheap. The citizens of the Japanese towns had neither time nor place for the large pseudo-Chinese, Confucian moralising scenes which decorated the large screens in the halls of their rulers. They wanted dispensible up-to-the-minute pictures of the famous Kabuki theatre actors, of the most popular courtesans in their newest dresses and styles. These served as fashion plates, and fashion conscious ladies throughout the whole of Japan eagerly awaited them. Judging from the quantity produced they all seem to have enjoyed salacious prints which showed their rulers riotously entangled with the darlings of the prostitute quarters. As a result, the Government imposed a censorship. Following the craze for travel they found a new world of artistic delight in the endless fantasies which their artists wove around Japanese landscape from one end of the islands to the other. The output of these artists was truly prodigious. Competition for the public favour was intense and kept them on their toes. For nearly three centuries the commoners supported these prolific designers, their impresarios and the skilled workmen who translated their ideas into such accurate impressions. They demanded of them always something new and original; they were content with only the very highest artistic and technical standards. A small New Year's card intended for private circulation was often a gem, its delicate printing embellished with gold, silver and blind printing. A huge landscape print in bold sweeps of colour could create a brilliant design from a familiar scene and sell in thousands until the blocks were worn out. Even now one can appreciate the revelation such prints must have been to Western painters dissatisfied with their own traditions and seeking new solutions to their problems of line and colour.

233 A so-called 'primitive' print by Kwaiget-sudo Anchi. Her dress has the design of a poet with fragments of poems in cursive script, c 1714. Coloured by hand in buff, tan, yellow and lilac.

234 Wood block print of an actor in a female role by Sharaku, 1794.

Of all the arts of the East, the Japanese colour print movement is the least easy to represent by a few examples. A large proportion of the many thousands of designs have originality and most of the hundreds of artists had their own personalities. The whole art is characterized by a restless seeking for new and original themes with which to capture the fickle market. The early 'primitive' prints have their own bold and vigorous use of line and simple colours often added by hand (*plate* 233). An actor print by Sharaku (*plate* 234), a group of courtesans

235 Colour print of Shinagawa by Hiroshige (1797-1858) taken from the series 'Fifty Three Stations of the Tokaido Highway'.

by Utamaro (*plate* 232), and a landscape by Hiroshige (*plate* 235) or Hokusai (*plate* 236), these represent only a tiny proportion of the highlights.

However, this disgression has taken us for a moment away from the main lines of development of painting. Painters continued to make the large screens which are such a feature of late Japanese art. The Kanō school was the 'official school', lavishly patronized by the Tokugawa Shōguns. As the Shōgunal style of painting it became popular throughout the country in the houses of the lesser feudal nobility who aped their masters. The kind of snobbism which brings fame and wealth even to a second rate painter of the royal family in Great Britain, acted in Japan in the sphere of Chinese style painting. The school itself split up into a number of branches and its pupils are legion. Kanō Tanyū (1602-1674) is the archtype of the school. The dictators heaped honour and rewards on him and he received some

244

236 Landscape colour print by Hokusai (1760-1849), one of a series ' Thirty six Views of Mount Fuji'.

of the most important commissions for the decoration of the castles. Confucian moralising subjects, emphasising the need for order in government, were popular. The brushwork is stiff and with a studied rather than an inherent power. Only the gold backgrounds some-times used gave the style a decorative brilliance. Paine has admir-ably summarized the work of this large school of painters: 'Art was to enoble man, to illustrate models of conduct, to serve in the purpose of good government, and to suggest virtues symbolically. This was a crushing programme, and art in the service of good government soon ceased to be great art.'

The Tosa family fortunes for a while were at a very low ebb. Technically they were the official painters to the old Kyoto court while the Kanō served the Edo dictators. However, a study of their painting in this period reveals a great deal of eclecticism and borrow-ing from all the traditions of the past. The true inheritors of the

Yamato-e, the native Japanese tradition with its love of colour and decorative effects and sweeping flat areas of colour, were not so much the Tosa painters as the Sōtatsu-Kōetsu-Kōrin group. Kōetsu (1558-1637) was the typical artist craftsman of the period, equally at home in the arts of calligraphy, pottery and lacquer. Living in the outskirts of Kyoto, he gathered around himself a whole group of like-minded artists and, although his calligraphy is very highly considered, he seems to have served mainly as an arbiter of taste. Sōtatsu, who may well have been related to Kōetsu, belonged to the same group. He was well versed in the traditions of the Tosa and had studied the great handscrolls of the Kamakura period. But he reinterpreted them in broad sweeps of colour and with a boldness which was quite new.

237 Pair of folding screens by Ogata Kōrin (1658-1716) in which a river and two plum trees are treated in a flat decorative style against a golden

It was left to Ogata Kōrin (1663-1743) to bring this decorative style to its climax in a number of breathtaking screens of combined natural and artificial splendour, simply conceived and boldly carried through. Against gold backgrounds he displays natural features such as trees, flowers and landscape. Everything is pressed to serve a decorative purpose which instead of being weak and pretty was, at the hands of this master, powerful and dramatic. Whatever violence he did to nature was justified by the magnificent effects he created. This is an art which is uniquely Japanese.

The school of Kōrin did not enjoy a long line of followers and apart from Hōitsu (1761-1828), few of even these produced any notable works. Only the greatest artists can prevent decorative art from

background. Note the combination of the schematic treatment of the river and the naturalism of the trees.

238 Detail from the 'Deer' scroll with paintings attributed to Sōtatsu (active first half of the seventeenth century) and calligraphy by Kōetsu (1558-1637). (p 246)

becoming merely pretty. However, other new forces were at work in the old capital of Kyoto. Maruyama Ōkyo (1733-95) founded a school which professed attachment to the old Chinese masters but was strongly influenced by the naturalism of Western art. This had filtered through via Nagasaki, especially in the form of illustrations to medical books. Ōkyo's work is meticulous and true to nature in many respects but it has a colourful grandeur and a breadth of imagination which raises it above mere truth to nature. His snow laden pine trees on a grand screen (*plate* 239) indulge in a basic naturalism which the man in the street could understand and admire as being something quite new but the whole concept is monumentally decorative in the best tradition of Japanese painting in his century. The naturalistic trend quickly died out in Japanese art circles as it did also in China after the Jesuits had introduced it.

Admirers of Chinese culture, the true sinophiles, found neither Maruyama's naturalism nor the studied Kanō styles satisfying outlets for their talents. To them Chinese painting meant the products of the *wên-jên*, the literary men. As we have mentioned, *wên-jên* in Japanese becomes *bun-jin* and their painting *bun-jin ga*. The free brushwork, impressionistic style, spiritual aims and subtle atmosphere of this style of Chinese painting appealed to the cultivated amateur. The Japanese literary painters were often, in true Chinese scholar traditions, also poets, and they often wrote their short stanzas on the paintings they made. The whole movement strikes a more sincere and personal note than the Kanō products of these centuries. Tra-

248

239 'Pine Trees in Snow', one of a pair of folding screens in colour on paper by Ōkyo (1733-95), a painter influenced by Western naturalism.

dition, as in China, demanded that the painter should be strictly amateur, painting purely for the expression of his soul. Whether they were in fact any more amateur than, say, our Olympic sportsmen is open to question. Certainly their basic approach was anti-naturalistic.

The movement started about 1700 and was firmly established half a century later by notable exponents like the poet painter Yōsa Buson (1716-1783) and Ike-no-Taiga (1723-1776). Both were versatile and eclectic in that they could paint in the Chinese Yüan-Ming styles as well as in the later Chinese Ch'ing dynasty individualistic modes. Their large works in the Yüan-Ming styles are sometimes a little formal and empty but their smaller paintings reveal a fine, free imaginative use of brush, ink and colour, a boldness in the exploitation of the sensitive Eastern materials, and equal anything the Chinese were doing at the period. Uragami Gyokudō (1715-1820) is one of the great masters of the style and there can be little doubt that many of these *bun-jin* painters were greatly influenced by the Chinese individualists, but, although they took the style from the Chinese, they then carried it to greater lengths than did any of the Chinese themselves. Gyokudō seems to have modelled his life on painters like the Chinese Chêng Hsieh (famous for his bamboos). He gave up an official position and spent his time in travel as an itinerant musician, painting and writing about his native land as he explored its many beauties. The tradition of Gyokudō's work is frankly Chinese, but the observation is more warm, friendly and intimate than that of the Chinese masters of the period. His imagination, too, is more fertile

240 'Mountain Landscape in Changing Weather' by Uragami Gyokudō (1745-1820) a Japanese *bun-jin* painter. He owes much to the Chinese individualist painters of the eighteenth century but the impressionistic ink approach is very personal.

241 Japanese Old Kutani ware plate of enamelled porcelain decorated with a mountain landscape. The Chinese influence is here very strong.
242 Japanese Kakiemon ware octagonal bowl in enamelled porcelain decorated with a flowering tree motif. Tokugawa period. (p 252)

and his brushwork shows a more fearless determination to explore all the possibilities of the medium. By the end of the eighteenth century the Japanese were leading the East in the field of painting. The Chinese had nothing comparable to offer.

The ceramics fall into two main groups. In one are porcelains which take their inspiration from the great tradition of China and to a lesser degree of Korea and in the second group are those which show the native taste and were mainly used for the tea ceremony. Altogether this was the great age of ceramics and estimates of the number of different kilns and potters are as high as ten thousand.

The porcelains which take their inspiration from China were (at least according to tradition) introduced by a Korean captured during Hideyoshi's campaigns. They were all made in the southern island of Kyūshū and fall into a few broad groups. Old Kutani (*plate* 241) wares were made during the second half of the seventeenth century, most of them technically inferior to the Chinese enamelled wares which inspired them. They often have warped shapes and impure white backgrounds, but these imperfections contrive to give them their life and differentiate them from the studied perfection of their Chinese ancestors. The predominant colour is a strikingly bright green enamel and the designs have a freedom and boldness (admirers of Chinese porcelain would call it coarseness) which is very refreshing. The Japanese tendency is often to splash one single pictorial motif over the whole of the surface in gay abandon. Sometimes geometric designs are repeated over the whole of the surface much as they would be on a textile. Both these decorative tendencies are quite un-Chinese.

The clay for porcelain was first found in the neighbourhood of Arita in Kyūshū Island and this name covers a wide range of wares. The easiest to distinguish are Kakiemon, Imari and Nabeshima. The Kakiemon family produced such a perfect white glaze on which to display their delicate enamels that even the Chinese admired them and they certainly won the admiration of the West when they reached such centres as Meissen.

Imari is the name of the port from which many Arita wares were exported to the West and it has come to describe the highly decorated less-perfect pieces which were sent to Europe. Some of these with under-glaze blue and over-glaze enamel decorations can be very florid while others have decorations inspired by the strange ships and foreigners which could be seen at Nagasaki.

The finest of all the Arita wares are those known as Nabeshima, from the name of the local noble family for whose exclusive use they were supposed to be made. They were manufactured from 1722 onwards. The porcelain of these is a fine milky white with under-glaze blue sometimes used, alone or with the addition of enamel colours. The drawing of the designs is always outstanding, for only the best were allowed to leave the kiln to serve the tables of the wealthy Japanese families. The designs are typically Japanese in that a single motif is often used pictorially over the whole surface of the plate, sometimes falling over the edge and continuing on the outside. Often whole sets were manufactured with subtle differences frequently introduced to give interest and variety. The designs are seldom dull or repetitious and always have that thoughtful appreciation of detail which characterizes the Japanese artist potter.

243 Japanese Imari (Arita) export ware plate in blue, black, red and gold enamelled porcelain with a Dutch ship design. Tokugawa period.

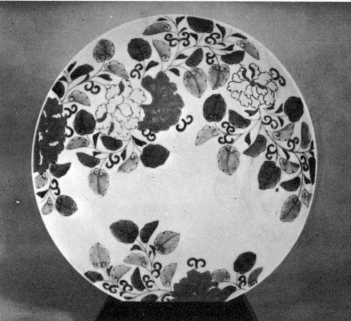

244, 245 Inside and side view of a Japanese Nabeshima (Arita) ware dish in underglaze blue and overglaze enamelled porcelain. Tokugawa period.

The second main category of ceramics was made in and around Kyoto. Of a number of artist potters the best known is Ninsei, who was active in the early Edo period and died c 1695. His enamelled pottery wares make a strong appeal to the Japanese who see in them an extension into ceramics of the native *Yamato-e* school of painting. He would sometimes apply them on a jet-black lacquer-like background. Certainly he seems to have had lacquer work in mind when he catered for the taste of patrons who admired rich sumptuous effects. At its best his work has that peculiarly Japanese gift of combining natural motifs with artificiality. At its worst it is hopelessly overwrought and frankly gaudy. Nevertheless, the use of clay as a means of expression of personality by an artist, and the patronage and position these craftsmen achieved in Japan, was quite unknown in China.

This type of overglaze decoration influenced the makers of the tea ceremony ware throughout the following centuries and many early pieces, known as Old Kiyomizu wares from the name of the pottery market on the way to the Kiyomizu Temple in Kyoto, have survived. They are generally in a style related to the work of Ninsei.

A number of eminent potters carried on the tradition initiated by Ninsei. The artist who did most to elevate the craft to the rank of a recognised art was Kenzan (1664-1743), a wealthy gentleman potter who often called on his famous brother, the painter Kōrin, to decorate his wares. The skill of his work lies in the balance he often achieved between the vessel and its ornamentation. One sees in this kind of work a preference for bizarre shapes which tend towards the sculptural. The cross between enamelled wares and pottery for the tea ceremony is not the most attractive of Japanese wares but it expressed one facet of the spirit of the age.

One of the features of the Tokugawa period is the way in which high standards of taste seem to have permeated right the way down through society. This is seen in the quality of dress design to which the colour print artists turned their talents. Women's dress had been an important art form in other periods (notably during Fujiwara times) but then only at a time when a relatively restricted noble society could enjoy the luxury of fine costume. The bourgeois ladies

246 Fan-shaped plate of enamelled porcelain with decoration of blue flowers and grasses by Kenzan (1664-1743), a typical artist potter product unique to Japan.

of the Tokugawa were just as wealthy and demanding as their noble forebears, but were also more frank in their tastes and more extravagant than their Fujiwara predecessors. We know how the prints carried news of *demi-monde* style and of the rapid changes of fashions. An outmoded hair-style or fabric could ruin a print. It seems that artists of both the decorative and print movements found common ground in fashion design. Certainly the originality, the breadth and daring, and the immense variety signify the work of artists rather than of hack textile designers.

A heady atmosphere of bravado hangs over much Tokugawa art. The economy of the period to some degree influenced the textile designers' work and by restricting materials available to them, stimulated their ingenuity. When rich Chinese brocades were prohibited by law or no longer imported, the ladies were forced to turn to Japanese materials. To compensate for the loss of gold and silver the Japanese developed techniques for dyeing their patterns. They used tie-dyeing for small all-over designs as well as for broad patterns and they often further embellished these with embroidery. The Government from time to time passed laws aimed at preventing the merchants from enjoying the wealthy things they could easily afford but this only inspired their designers to create new and more splendid effects by simple means.

By the end of the seventeenth century two new techniques were introduced – the use of stencils for block printing and a rice-paste resist dyeing technique perfected by Miyazaki Yūzensai about 1700. This technique was inspired by batik work from the East Indies and in combination with others or alone it dominated the fabrics of the next two centuries. At the end of the eighteenth century wood block printing came into use to satisfy the demands for speed and economy of manufacture.

Apart from the techniques of cloth manufacture the Japanese often used these materials in highly imaginative ways. They sometimes visualised a dress as a single pictorial unit on which to splash one magnificent motif in the most daring manner. It was the sheer force of combined luxury and vigour which enabled them to combine what one might have thought gaudy and irreconcilable into a grand design.

247 Stencil dyed and embroidered robe worn by Keisho-in, mother of Tsunayoshi, the fifth Tokugawa Shōgun.

248 Japanese lacquer *inrō*, or box to hang from the sash in Japanese dress and used for personal items. The design in gold lacquer of a courtesan is taken from the colour prints. Nineteenth century.

In lacquer, another luxury product, the craftsmen seemed to be aiming at an effect which combined the sparkle of jewellery and the interest of pictorial design. In this field too it was the innovations of the Momoyama period which formed the basis on which the Tokugawa strove to create ever more decorative, unusual, varied works. Their twin main interests of man and nature and a cunning skill in applying these to what is essentially one of the most decorative and artificial mediums created countless objects of undeniable taste and elegance. As in the other crafts we see a restless search for what is new and original. The Chinese custom of finding a successful formula and sticking to it would, for a Japanese, represent a failure of the imagination. They were always ready to experiment. One senses that their customers always wanted something different. The highest standards of craftsmanship distinguished their work. We illustrate it by an *inrō*, a small box carried from a sash tucked into the waist band. It is only one of many thousands of such boxes in as many different shapes, materials and designs (*plate* 248).

249 Japanese ornamental sword, *tsuba*, in copper with gold and silver design of a rock and blossoming tree. Tokugawa period.

However, it is perhaps in the metalwork and small carvings worked from ivory and wood that one can best appreciate the skill, taste, ingenuity and artistic observation which seems to have flowed through almost every aspect of life during these centuries. The student who becomes absorbed in this flood of miniature art is in danger of drowning. For instance, the manufacture of *tsuba*, or sword guards, and other sword furniture absorbed the energies of countless metal workers throughout the land. These *tsuba* had by now surrendered all pretence of practical use and served as gifts from local lords to officials from the Edo court or just between friends. They became jewellery like in splendour and attention to detail. Of the many thousands of guards in different techniques and designs from ateliers all over Japan it seems invidious to choose only one to represent so many. However, the guard in *plate* 249 shows some of the characteristics of Tokugawa art. The gold and silver on copper is a favourite ploy in which a base metal offsets precious materials. Here again is the same careful observation and delight in nature and the love of the pictorial. Here too is workmanship which can have few equals throughout the world. It shows the gift of fitting a satisfying design into a difficult shape, a challenge which the Japanese have always seemed to welcome. The ability to uphold such standards even in the smallest object can be seen in *plate* 250 which is shown in its original size enlarged four times. It is an *ōjime*, a button used to keep the cords of an *inrō* tight and thus the box securely closed. The enlargement shows the skill which has gone into designing for such a small compass. And such objects were produced in their thousands with repetitions found only very rarely indeed.

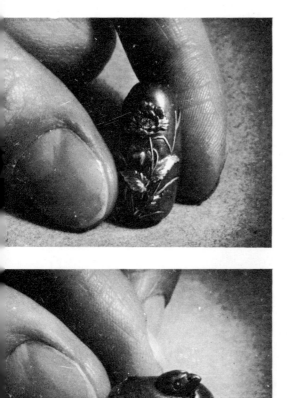

250, 251   Two Japanese metal *ōjme*, or buttons, used to keep the *inrō* cord closed tight (plate 248). Many thousands of such miniature masterpieces of observation exist. Japanese Tokugawa period c 1800.

A final tribute to the countless craftsmen of the period comes from the equally large field of *netsuke*, the large button-like objects used in Japanese dress to hold the sash for the *inrō* firmly under the belt. The earliest date from the sixteenth century, but most surviving examples are from the eighteenth and nineteenth centuries. Every possible material was used to make them, but wood and ivory are the most common. Humans and animals are favourite themes and for some the metal workers were pressed into service. The latter made mostly *manjū*, or bun-like buttons with ivory on the outside and metal in the centre. In these charming objects of infinite care and skill the talents of the Japanese carvers and sculptors was fully exploited. Again it is impossible to give more than a glimpse of these masterpieces of Liliputian art which have intrigued Western collectors for generations.

In 1868 a combination of internal and external pressures forced Japan out of her seclusion. Her art from that period onwards joined the main stream of world art.

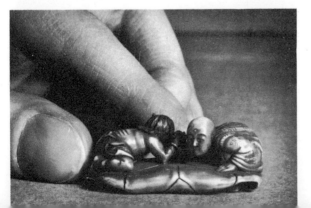

252, 253 Two Tokugawa Japanese carved ivory *netsuke* used at the waist end of the cord holding the *inrō* (plate 248). The degree of detail and fineness of workmanship in such small objects provide a continual source of delight.

Postscript

The modern histories of China, Japan and Korea illustrate how the hard facts of modern international power politics affected three Far Eastern countries in very different ways. China in the nineteenth century was the first to feel the thrust of the West and various European powers rapidly ate into her economic, cultural and at times military independence. In the 1850's America forced Japan to open her doors to the West and a similar or even a worse fate of complete domination might well have befallen her had she not shown such energy, far-sightedness and courage. Korea became a colony of resurgent imperialist Japan which had quickly learned the rules from the West. Korea was only released after the last war.

In China, already by the late eighteenth century, the rise of population and the increasing venality of the administration was already creating serious internal problems. The Confucian straight-jacket blinded the Manchus to the prospect of any change, however necessary, and their calm assumption of the superiority of Chinese culture left them powerless in the face of the encroachments of Western powers, notably of the British. Neither Manchu nor Chinese administrators could appreciate the danger inherent in frustrating the economic ambitions of nineteenth century Western mercantile nations and a series of wars led to much of China being divided up into spheres of interest controlled by the various Western nations interested in the area. However, unlike in India, no Western nation ever took over the actual running of large areas of the country. They were content to establish extra-territorial rights in the ports they occupied and then proceed to milk the hinterlands. From the mid-nineteenth century onwards they had an economic stranglehold on the country.

Japan's fate was very different. Internally the ruling class found itself in serious debt to the merchants while the unfortunate peasants were oppressed by both merchants and the samurai alike. The declining feudal system could not adapt itself to the demands of modern mercantilism. The long-lived Tokugawa régime fell before three opponents, a group of strong but dissatisfied lords living mainly in the west of the islands, the irresistible force of foreign demands to open the country and the resurgence of the Emperor in Kyoto as a real force in political life. The Americans played the key role in forcing Japan at gun point out of her sleep of two and a half centuries. Perry made Japan sign an agreement in 1854 and similar agreements followed with other Western nations. The failure of the Tokugawa to resist foreign threats led to its speedy downfall and to the restoration of the Emperor in 1867-8.

For a while it looked as if Japan, like China, would disintegrate before the power of the avaricious West, but by skilful diplomacy she was able to rid herself of the worse aspects of the unequal treaties and establish herself as a modern country based on Western style industrialism backed by Western style armed forces. She then set out on a course of empire building in the East of which the last act has only recently been played. The defeat of Russia in the war of 1904-5 set the seal on Japan's independence and brought her full and equal membership of the circle of great powers. The effort she put into Westernisation reminds the historian of a similar effort in the sixth century when Japan acquired Chinese culture.

The Japanese had long regarded Korea as their sphere of interest — as evidenced by the invasions of Hideyoshi at the end of the sixteenth century. After the Russo-Japanese war the Japanese felt free to renew their ambitions in Korea, and, outdoing the West in their thoroughness, they made the Korean peninsular into a Japanese colony. From 1910 followed thirty-five years of Japanese rule which was efficient if at times somewhat harsh. The Japanese militarists, however, did not prove good administrators and they completely failed to destroy the deep Korean desire for independence and bring about the integration of Korea and Japan.

During this century it is fair to say that Japan has led the Eastern world in the arts. During the Meiji period (1868-1912) an initial rejection of their own culture and all things Japanese was followed by a swing in the opposite direction under the guidance of the American scholar Fenollosa (1853-1908) and Ōkakura Kakuzō, both of whom tried to awaken the Japanese to the need to preserve the ancient treasures in danger of being disregarded. At the same time they tried to revitalize traditional artistic methods. In the latter only Tessai (1836-1924) seems to have succeeded but he was a true Chinese style artist who belonged more to the previous period. Only his vigour, eccentricity and seemingly undisciplined brushwork pointed towards the new trends of art. The early painters in Western style amazed the Japanese of their day but they do not to-day inspire us.

These Western style painters quickly entered the international field and went to European art centres, notably Paris, to study. Some of them, like Takeuchi Seihō (1864-1942) impressed Western audiences with their seeming sleight of hand with a brush and ink in the Eastern style and tried to effect a synthesis of East and West. A few like Umehara Ryūsabarō studied under great masters like Renoir, understood the problems facing the artists of their time and added their own contribution to Western art. Nowadays, exponents of almost every European and American style are to be found in Japan but as yet one doubts whether a really great oil painter has appeared.

However, in the field of calligraphy they have produced many fine artists. This is an abstract art with which they are completely familiar and their products have influenced Western calligraphic styles of painting. The greatest contribution of modern Japanese artists is in the field of wood-block printing, an old technique now brilliantly revived (*plates* 254-6). The whole of this century has seen a succession of artists who have been steadily growing in vitality and originality. Most of them work in international modes but are making their own very individual contribution. The designs, colours and materials have all the subtlety of past centuries allied to the variety and imagination of the twentieth century.

254 Modern Japanese ink and colour print, 'Songs', by Shiko Munakata, who
takes his inspiration from old Buddhist prints.
255 Japanese print in black and white, 'Ship at Rest', by Fumio Kitaoka, 1952.

256 Japanese ink and colour print on paper, 'Garden with Stone and
Sand', by Ōkiie Hashimoto, 1961. An entirely modern interpretation of
one of the most traditional themes in Eastern painting.

257 'Light and Darkness' by Shunso Machi. An example of contemporary Japanese calligraphy an art form in which the Japanese from long experience lead and influence the rest of the world.

The craft potters flourish as never before and their works continue to influence pottery throughout the world. In the last ten years the influence of Japan on architects and industrial designers has increased tenfold. There would be support for a claim that Japan leads the world in architectural invention and daring.

In China, a number of painters continued the traditions of *wên-jên* painting and some, like Ju Peon and Ch'i Pai-shih achieved considerable international success. However, more important are a number of outstanding landscape painters like Fu Pao-shih (born 1904) (*plate* 258), Chiang Song-yan (born 1898) and Sung Chi-hsiang (born 1917). These men work in the best tradition of Chinese ink and water colours. Although the State supports many schools with their Western style departments, the demands of political expediency have prevented Chinese artists in the Western style from exploring the new visual artistic possibilities which have so absorbed the energies of international painters in this century. Western style painting in China has tended to be dull oil painting of political subjects drawn in the most naturalistic manner. This is a type of work which all Communist countries seem to find it necessary to support for a time. On the credit side is the tremendous impetus which the régime is giving to archaeological research and to the creation of new museums. The craft works are also being encouraged so that, compared with the generally low standards of porcelain manufacture in the late nineteenth century, the great factories are now encouraged to produce good quality wares, some of which are very passable reproductions of eighteenth century monochromes. As yet it can hardly be claimed that a twentieth century ceramic style has emerged.

There also exists a considerable body of Chinese painters working in the West. They are constantly experimenting with new and often exciting ways of expression but a discussion of their very varied work belongs to a book on modern Western painting.

Korea had hardly emerged from her troubles of this century under the Japanese when the country was split between Communist and non-Communist. It is still impossible to indicate any individual new trends but occasionally a Korean artist like Kam Zin-choon comes to Europe, studies there, and produces original works in the

267

258 Large landscape in ink and faint colour on paper by Fu Pao-shih, contemporary Chinese painting in a traditional style going back to Tao Chi.

traditional medium (*plate* 259). It is safe to predict that within the next few years Korean artists of great ability will appear.

The problems facing all Eastern artists are fundamentally the same. They are now all in the full stream of international art. What is created one day in New York is caught up the next in Paris and Tokyo. Yet the Japanese and Koreans have yet completely to integrate their skill and tastes into this stream, while the Chinese have not yet been allowed to do so. When they do, and certainly they all will, the world will be the richer and our art more lively and varied. The Eastern artistic genius has always had and still has very much to offer.

259 Hanging scroll, 'Bird on a Branch', by Kam Zin-choon, ink on paper, contemporary Korean, influenced by Chinese individualists like Chu Ta (plate 221).

Text References

page

24 W. Watson, *China*, London 1961, p 154

54 G.St.G.M. Gompertz, in *Oriental Art*, Vol VII No 1, p 13

148 O. Siren, *Chinese Painting: Leading Masters and Principles*, London 1956, Vol II p 115

160 D. Seckel, *E Makimono*, London 1959, p 15

162 P. C. Swann, *Introduction to the Arts of Japan*, Oxford 1958, p 104

168 J. Ayers, 'Some Characteristic Wares of the Yüan Dynasty' in *Transactions of the Oriental Ceramic Society* Vol 29 pp 69-86, to which I am indebted for much of the information used on Yüan ceramics.

183 A. Lane 'The Arts of the Ming Dynasty' catalogue of the Oriental Ceramic Society, 1957

205 G.St.G.M. Gompertz, introduction to the catalogue of an exhibition, 'The National Art Treasures of Korea', The Arts Council, London 1961

245 R. Paine and A.C. Soper, *The Art and Architecture of Japan*, London 1956, p 107

	C H I N A	K O R E A	J A P A N
c.1550	Capital at Cheng-chou SHANG-YIN		
c.1350	at DYNASTY		JOMON
c.1150	An-yang		PERIOD
	CHOU DYNASTY		
722	Beginning of break-up	NAN-SHAN	
480		PERIOD	
221	Warring States Period		
206	CH'IN DYNASTY		
c.200	HAN DYNASTY (FORMER)		
8 BC/AD	– – – – – – – – – – – – –	LO-LANG PERIOD – – – – – –	– – YAYOI – – – –
25	(LATER)		PERIOD
220			
c.300	THREE KINGDOMS		
318	PERIOD		
c.370			GREAT TOMBS
386			PERIOD
420	SUNG D'NASTY / NORTHERN WEI DYNASTY	KOGURYO / PAEKCHE / SILLA	
479			
501	CH'I D'NASTY		
552	LIANG D'NASTY / EAST AND WEST WEI DYNASTIES		
589	CH'EN D'NASTY / NORTH CH'I AND CHOU DYNASTIES		ASUKA
618	SUI DYNASTY		
645			NARA
794	T'ANG		KONIN
907		SILLA	
918	FIVE DYNASTIES PERIOD / LIAO DYNASTY		HEIAN
960	SUNG DYNASTY		FUJIWARA
1185	/ CHIN DYNASTY	KORYO	KAMAKURA
1271	YUAN DYNASTY		ASHIKAGA (MUROMACHI)
1337			
1868			
1392	MING DYNASTY		(AZUCHI)—MOMOYAMA PERIOD
1578		YI DYNASTY	(EDO) TOKUGAWA
1616			
1644	CH'ING DYNASTY		
1867			MEIJI
1910			
1912	REPUBLIC	CHOSEN	
1949	PEOPLE'S CHINA (Nationalist China on Formosa)		

List of illustrations

36 Ordos bronze horse trapping. Musée Cernuschi, Paris.
37 Han dynasty gilt bronze bear. British Museum, London.
38 Early Han dynasty decorated clay tile from Chin-ts'un, Honan province. Wadsworth Atheneum, Hartford, Connecticut. Photo: The Asia Society, New York.
39 Han dynasty decorated lacquer bowl. Seattle Art Museum.
40 Han dynasty lacquer painted basket from Lolang, Korea. National Museum of Korea, Seoul. Photo: courtesy of Heibonsha Kabushiki Kaisha, Tokyo.
41 Part of Han dynasty painted tile. Courtesy, Museum of Fine Arts, Boston.
42 Detail of a late Han dynasty tomb wall-painting in Wang Tu, Hupei province.
43 Han dynasty gold belt buckle from Lolang, Korea. Academy of Arts, Honolulu.
44 Middle Jōmon pot. Tokyo University.
45 Middle Jōmon clay figurine. Tokyo National Museum.
46 Late Jōmon clay figurine. Tokyo National Museum.
47 Tomb of Emperor Nintoku near Osaka.
48 Old Tomb period Haniwa figurine. Photo: Asia Society, New York.
49 Old Tomb period Haniwa warrior. Photo: Asia Society, New York.
50 Old Tomb period Haniwa monkey. Photo: Asia Society, New York.
51 Detail from a fifth-sixth century tomb wall-painting at T'ung-kou, Manchuria.
52 Colossal figures in Buddhist cave-temples at Yün-kang, Shansi province, 460-80 AD. Photo: courtesy of C. Arthaud.
53 Large standing Buddha from cave 18, Yün-kang, Shansi, 460-80 AD. Photo: courtesy of C. Arthaud.
54 Minor statues at Yün-kang, Shansi. 460-80 AD. Photo: courtesy of C. Arthaud.
55 Bodhisattva in the later style at Yün-kang, Shansi. Photo: courtesy of C. Arthaud.
56 Part of main cave-temple with colossal figures in T'ang dynasty style at Lung-mên, Honan province. Photo: courtesy of C. Arthaud.
57 Stone seated Bodhisattva in late Northern Wei dynasty style from Lung-mên, Honan. Courtesy, Museum of Fine Arts, Boston.
58 View of third-fifth centuries Buddhist cave-temples site at Bamiyan, Afghanistan. Photo: courtesy of C. Arthaud.
59 View of the west Chinese cave-temples site at Mai-chi-shan begun under the Northern Wei dynasty. Photo: courtesy of C. Arthaud.
60 Gilt bronze Maitreya dated 477 AD. Courtesy of the Metropolitan Museum of Art, New York.
61 Sixth century Chinese gilt bronze altarpiece. Courtesy of the Metropolitan Museum of Art, New York.
62 Chinese gilt bronze shrine dated 518 AD. Musée Guimet, Paris.
63 Northern Wei dynasty painted terracotta horse. Royal Ontario Museum of Art.
64 Section of 'Admonitions of the Imperial Instructress' attributed to Ku K'ai-chih (c 344-c 406). British Museum, London.
65 Fourth-sixth century Yüeh type toilet box. Ashmolean Museum, Oxford.
66 Third century Chinese painted pottery attendant. Ashmolean Museum, Oxford.
67 Third-fourth century Chinese stone chimera. William Rockhill Nelson Gallery of Art, Atkins Museum of Fine Arts, Kansas City.
68 Fifth-sixth century Chinese stone chimera. University Museum, Philadelphia.
69 Temple wall-painting of c 500 AD at Tun-huang, Chinese Turkestan. Photo: courtesy of C. Arthaud.
70 Detail of scenes engraved on the side of a Chinese limestone sarcophagus of c 525 AD. William Rockhill Nelson Gallery of Art, Atkins Museum of Fine Arts.
71 Two painted clay figures at Tun-huang. Photo: courtesy of C. Arthaud.
72 The Kudara Kannon. Hōryū-ji, Nara.
73 Fifth-sixth century Sillan gold crown. Museum für Völkerkunde, Munich.
74 Eighth-ninth century Sillan earthenware bowl.
75 Fifth-sixth century Sillan pottery figure. Academy of Arts, Honolulu.

109 T'ang dynasty gold headdress. The Minneapolis Institute of Arts.
110 A pair of T'ang dynasty painted clay female dancers. The Mount Collection, London. Photo: R. Fortt.
111 T'ang dynasty painted clay figure. The Ingram Collection, Cirencester, Glos., England.
112 T'ang dynasty fragment of embroidered silk. British Museum, London.
113 Two T'ang dynasty silver and parcel gilt bowls with covers. Seattle Art Museum.
114 Secret wooden statue of Nyoin Kannon. 826-36. Kanshin-ji, Osaka.
115 Early Heian period painting of a Fūdo. Myōo-in, Koya-san, Japan.
116 Late T'ang dynasty white porcelain cup and vase. Ashmolean Museum, Oxford.
117 Tenth century Yüeh ware incised jar, or amphora. Ashmolean Museum, Oxford.
118 'Seeking the Tao in the Autumn Mountains' attributed to Chü-jan (tenth century). United Museums and Libraries, Palace Museum Division, Formosa.
119 Wood gilt Amida Buddha by Jōcho (died 1057). Byōdō-in Temple, Kyoto.
120 Sung dynasty *ting* ware bird-headed ewer. British Museum, London.
121 Sung dynasty incised bowl and toilet box of *ch'ing-pai* ware. Ashmolean Museum, Oxford.
122 Sung dynasty *ting* ware tea or wine pot. Fitzwilliam Museum, Cambridge.
123 Sung dynasty Tz'u-chou ware jar. British Museum, London.
124 Sung dynasty *chün* ware bowl and jar. British Museum, London.
125 Sung dynasty Northern Celadon bowl. Ashmolean Museum, Oxford.
126 Sung dynasty decorated *chien* ware vase. Ashmolean Museum, Oxford.
127 Sung dynasty Lung-ch'üan celadon vase. Fitzwilliam Museum, Cambridge.
128 Sung dynasty *kuan* ware bowl. Ashmolean Museum, Oxford.
129 Liao dynasty green glazed vase. Ashmolean Museum, Oxford.
130 Sung dynasty *ju* ware vase. Collection of Mrs A. Clark, Fulmer, Bucks, England.
131 Liao dynasty seated ceramic lohan. University Museum of Philadelphia.
132 Sung dynasty wooden Kuan-yin. Courtesy, Museum of Fine Arts, Boston.
133 'Travelling Among the Mountains and Streams' by Fan Kuan (fl. 900-1030). Formosa.
134 'Five-coloured Parakeet on the Branch of a Blossoming Apricot Tree' by Hui-tsung (1082-1135). Fogg Art Museum, Harvard University.
135 Landscape on a silk fan by Ma Yüan (fl. 1190-1230). Courtesy, Museum of Fine Arts, Boston.
136 Part of a landscape scroll by Hsia Kuei (fl. 1180-1230). United Museums and Libraries, Palace Museum Division, Formosa.
137 'Six Persimmons' by Mu Ch'i (fl. 1200-55). Daitoku-ji, Kyoto.
138 Koryō dynasty celadon wine pot with incised and raised design. Ducksoo Palace Museum of Fine Arts, Seoul.
139 Koryō dynasty celadon wine pot with inlaid decoration. Ducksoo Palace Museum of Fine Arts, Seoul.
140 Koryō dynasty silver ewer with gold decoration. Courtesy, Museum of Fine Arts, Boston.
141 Koryō dynasty celadon vase with underglaze iron oxide decoration. Ducksoo Palace Museum of Fine Arts, Seoul.
142 Koryō dynasty celadon bowl with inlaid design. Ducksoo Palace Museum of Fine Arts, Seoul.
143 Eleventh-twelfth century figure of a monk at Mai-chi-shan in west China. Photo: courtesy of C. Arthaud.
144 Coloured wood figure of Mūchaku by Unkei (1142-1212). Kōfuku-ji, Nara.
145 Portrait of Shigemori by Takanobu (1142-1205). Jingō-ji, Kyoto.
146 Kamakura period icon of Amida Buddha descending from paradise. Zenrin-ji, Kyoto.
147 Portrait of Myōe Shōnin meditating, attributed to Jōnin (thirteenth century). Kōzan-ji, Kyoto.

276

181 Group of Ming dynasty monochrome and enamel decorated pottery. Private collections.
182 Fifteenth century Chinese cloisonné censer.
183 Late Ming dynasty *blanc-de-chine* figure of Bodhidharma. Collection of Mr and Mrs R. Palmer, Twyford, Berks., England.
184 Ming dynasty ivory figure of a seated official. H. M. The King of Sweden.
185 Ming dynasty carved red lacquer cup and stand. Collection of Sir Percival and Lady David, London.
186 Ming dynasty Hsüan-tê period (1426-35) Imperial table of carved red lacquer. Collection of Mr Fritz Löw-Beer, New York.
187 Rear view of early fifteenth century Chinese Imperial lacquer painted cabinet. Collection of Mr Fritz Löw-Beer, New York.
188 Landscape by Shūbun (fl. first half of the fifteenth century). Seattle Art Museum.
189 Winter landscape by Sesshū (1420-1506). National Museum, Tokyo.
190 'Amano Hashidate' by Sesshū (1420-1506). National Commission for the Protection of Cultural Properties, Tokyo.
191 Seascape by Sesson (1504-89). Collection of Mr Nomura, Kyoto.
192 Waterfall by Kanō Motonobu (1475-1550). Yamato Bunkakan, Nara.
193 Landscape on one of a pair of screens by Sōami (died 1525). Daitoku-ji, Kyoto.
194 Sung dynasty *chien* ware bowl. Ashmolean Museum, Oxford.
195 'Sage in Meditation' by Kang Hui-an (1419-65). National Museum of Korea, Seoul.
196 Early Korean blue-and-white jar. Seattle Art Museum.
197 The Himeji Castle, Momoyama Period.
198 'Plum Trees by a Riverside', a pair of screens attributed to Kanō Eitoku (1543-90). Daitoku-ji, Kyoto.
199 'Flowering Plum Trees', four sliding doors in the style of Kanō Sanraku (1559-1635). Daitoku-ji, Kyoto.
200 'Pine Forest', a pair of screens by Hasegawa Tōhaku (1539-1610). National Museum, Tokyo.
201 'Raku' tea-bowl made by Chōjiro (fl. 1576-92).
202 Momoyama period Oribe ware teapot. Seattle Art Museum.
203 Momoyama period square dish of Grey Shino Ware. Seattle Art Museum.
204 Momoyama period embroidered Noh theatre costume. National Museum Tokyo.
205 Detail of a Momoyama Kōdai-ji lacquer table top. National Museum Tokyo.
206 Ch'ing dynasty K'ang-hsi period (1622-1722) *famille verte* plate. Ashmolean Museum, Oxford.
207 Ch'ing dynasty *famille noire* vase. Victoria and Albert Museum, London.
208 Ch'ing dynasty *Ku-yüeh hsüan* ware *famille rose* vase. Ashmolean Museum, Oxford.
209 Ch'ing dynasty peach-bloom glazed vase. Ashmolean Museum, Oxford.
210 Eighteenth century imitation *kuan* ware brush washer. Ashmolean Museum, Oxford.
211 Ch'ing dynasty export ware armorial plate. Ashmolean Museum, Oxford.
212 Ch'ing dynasty *blanc-de-chine* figure of Kuan-yin. Ashmolean Museum, Oxford.
213 Ch'ing dynasty box of lacquer in three colours. Ashmolean Museum, Oxford.
214 Ch'ing dynasty Imperial throne of carved red lacquer. Victoria and Albert Museum, London.
215 Ch'ing dynasty carved jade brushpot. Ashmolean Museum, Oxford.
216 Ch'ing dynasty carved jade vase. Ashmolean Museum, Oxford.
217 Ch'ing dynasty gold inlaid imitation of an archaic bronze vessel. Ashmolean Museum, Oxford.
218 Landscape by Wang Hui (1632-1717). Musée Guimet, Paris.
219 Detail from 'Spring Morning' by Wang-Yüan-ch'i (1642-1715). Courtesy, Museum of Fine Arts, Boston.
220 Mountain landscape by K'un Ts'an (fl. 1655-75). The Fogg Museum of Art, Harvard University.

221 'Kingfisher on a Lotus Stalk' by Chu Ta (c. 1625-1700). K. Sumitomo Collection, Oiso, Japan.
222 River landscape dated 1703 by Tao Chi. Courtesy, Museum of Fine Arts, Boston.
223 Mountain landscape by Kung Hsien (c. 1617-89). The Drennovitz Collection, Switzerland.
224 Insects and calligraphy by Li Shan (first half of the eighteenth century). The author's collection, Oxford.
225 'The Diamond Mountains' by Chong Son (1676-1759). Jai-hyung Sohn Collection, Museum für Kunsthandwerk, Frankfurt.
226 Part of a landscape scroll by Yi In-man (1746-1825). Ducksoo Palace Museum of Fine Arts, Seoul.
227 'Steep Heights' by Kim Hong-do (born 1760). Jai-hyung Sohn Collection, Museum für Kunsthandwerk, Frankfurt.
228 'A Boating Party' by Sin Yun-bok (born 1758). Chun Hyung-pil Collection, Museum für Kunsthandwerk, Frankfurt.
229 Eighteenth century Korean porcelain jar with underglaze iron oxide decoration. Ducksoo Palace Museum of Fine Arts, Seoul.
230 Eighteenth century Korean porcelain bowl with underglaze blue decoration. Chun Hyung-pil Collection, Museum für Kunsthandwerk, Frankfurt.
231 Print of a Kabuki theatre actor by Kunisada (1786-1864). Ashmolean Museum, Oxford.
232 Print of two courtesans by Utamaro (1754-1806). Ashmolean Museum, Oxford.
233 'Primitive' print of a courtesan by Kwaigetsudo Anchi (fl. 1710's). The Art Institute of Chicago.
234 Print of an actor by Sharaku, 1794. Musée Guimet, Paris.
235 Print of Shinagawa by Hiroshige (1797-1858). British Museum, London.
236 Landscape print by Hokusai (1760-1849). British Museum, London.
237 River and two plum trees, pair of screens by Ōgata Kōrin (1658-1716). Atami Museum, Shizuoka-ken, Japan.
238 Detail from the 'Deer' scroll attributed to Sōtatsu and Kōetsu (1558-1632). Atami Museum, Shizuoka-ken, Japan.
239 'Pine Trees in Snow', one of a pair of screens by Ōkyo (1733-95). Collection of Mr Mitsui, Tokyo.
240 'Mountain Landscape in Changing Weather' by Uragami Gyokudō (1745-1820).
241 Seventeenth century Old Kutani ware plate. Seattle Art Museum.
242 Tokugawa period Kakiemon ware octagonal bowl. Seattle Art Museum.
243 Tokugawa period Imari, export, ware plate. Ashmolean Museum, Oxford.
244-5 Tokugawa period Nabeshima ware dish. Ashmolean Museum Oxford.
246 Fan-shaped plate of enamelled and decorated porcelain by Kenzan (1663-1743). Seattle Art Museum.
247 Togukawa period dyed and embroidered robe. National Museum, Tokyo.
248 Nineteenth century lacquer *inrō*. Ashmolean Museum, Oxford.
249 Tokugawa period inlaid copper *tsuba*. Ashmolean Museum, Oxford.
250-1 Two Tokugawa period carved ivory *netsuke*. Ashmolean Museum, Oxford.
252-3 Two Tokugawa period metal *ōjime*. Ashmolean Museum, Oxford.
254 Prints of 'Songs' by Shiko Munakata, 1956. Ashmolean Museum, Oxford.
255 Print, 'Ship at Rest', by Fumio Kitaoka, 1952. Ashmolean Museum, Oxford.
256 Print, 'Garden with Stone and Sand', by Ōkiie Hashimoto, 1961. Ashmolean Museum, Oxford.
257 Calligraphy, 'Light and Darkness' by Shunso Machi, contemporary. Japanese Embassy, London.
258 Contemporary Chinese landscape by Fu Pao-shih. Ashmolean Museum, Oxford.
259 Contemporary Korean scroll, 'Bird on a Branch' by Kam Zin-choon. Ashmolean Museum, Oxford.

Bibliography

The following is only a short bibliography including, where they exist, up-to-date books on the subject and in the main those most readily obtainable. A great deal of information is contained in periodicals such as *Artibus Asiae*, Ascona, *Oriental Art*, London, *Ars Orientalis*, Washington, *Bulletin of the Museum of Far Eastern Antiquities*, Stockholm and also of great importance are the Chinese and Japanese periodicals which are far more difficult to obtain and read. Any readers interested in reading more deeply will in time discover these for themselves.

Sir Leigh ASHTON and Basil GRAY, *Chinese Art*, London 1951

Ludwig BACHHOFER, *A Short History of Chinese Art*, New York 1946

Lawrence BINYON, *Painting in the Far East* (4th ed.), London 1949

L. BINYON and J. J. O'BRIAN SEXTON, *Japanese Colour Prints*, London 1923

Faubion BOWERS, *Japanese Theatre*, London 1934

Andrew BOYD, *Chinese Architecture*, London 1962

J. BUHOT, *Histoire des Arts du Japon* (Vol. I), Paris 1949

James CAHILL, *Chinese Painting*, Switzerland 1960

Schuyler CAMMANN, *China's Dragon Robes*, New York 1952

Catalogue of an Exhibition of Korean Art Treasures, London 1961

CHÊNG Tê-k'un, *Prehistoric China*, Cambridge, 1959

CHÊNG Tê-k'un, *Shang China*, Cambridge 1960

Chosen Government General *Chōsen Kōseki Zufu* (15 vols), Seoul 1915-35

William COHN, *Chinese Painting*, London 1957

E. CONZÉ, *Buddhism*, Oxford 1951

H. G. CREEL, *The Birth of China*, (Revised edition), New York, 1954

Leroy DAVIDSON, *The Lotus Sutra in Chinese Art*, New York 1954

A. DREXLER, *The Architecture of Japan*, New York 1955

G. ECKE, *Chinese Domestic Furniture* (Reprint), Rutland 1963

A. ECKHARDT, *A History of Korean Art*, London 1929

Sir Harry GARNER, *Oriental Blue and White*, London 1954

Sir Harry GARNER, *Chinese and Japanese Cloisonné Enamels*, London 1962

M. ST. G. M. GOMPERTZ, *Chinese Celadon Wares*, London 1958

Helen C. GUNSAULUS, *The Clarence Buckingham Collection of Japanese Prints*, Chicago 1955

Basil GRAY, *Early Chinese Pottery and Porcelain*, London 1953

Basil GRAY and John B. VINCENT, *Buddhist Cave Paintings at Tun-huang*, London 1959

René GROUSSETT, *Japon*, Paris 1930

René GROUSSETT, *The Rise and Splendour of the Chinese Empire*, London 1952

René GROUSSETT, *Chinese Art and Culture*, London 1959

Bo GYLLENSVÄRD, *T'ang Gold and Silver*, Stockholm 1957

L. HAJEK, A. HOFFMEISTER, E. RYCHTEROVA, *Contemporary Chinese Painting*, London 1961

S. Howard HANSFORD, *Chinese Jade Carving*, London 1950

S. Howard HANSFORD, *The Seligman Collection of Chinese Art*, (Vol. I *Chinese, Central Asian and Luristan Bronzes and Chinese Jades and Sculptures*), London 1957

J. HILLIER, *Japanese Masters of the Colour Print*, London 1955

J. HILLIER, *Hokusai*, London 1956

J. HILLIER, *The Japanese Print. A new Approach* London 1960

279

J. HILLIER, *Utamaro*, London 1961

R. L. HOBSON, *Chinese Pottery and Porcelain* (Two volumes), London 1915

R. L. HOBSON, *The Wares of the Ming Dynasty*, London 1923

R. L. HOBSON, *A Catalogue of Chinese Pottery and Porcelain in the Collection of Sir Percival David*, London 1934

R. L. HOBSON and W. P. YETTS, *The George Eumorfopoulos Collection* (9 vols), London 1925-1932

W. B. HONEY, *The Ceramic Art of China and other Countries of the Far East*, London 1945

W. B. HONEY, *Corean Pottery*, London 1947

Soame JENYNS, *Chinese Archaic Jades in the British Museum*, London 1951

Soame JENYNS, *Ming Pottery and Porcelain*, London 1953

Soame JENYNS, *Later Chinese Porcelain* (Revised edition), London 1959

H. L. JOLY, *Japanese Sword Guards*, London 1910

B. KARLGREN, *Yin and Chou Chinese Bronzes*, Museum of Far Eastern Antiquities Stockholm, 1936

George N. KATES, *Chinese Household Furniture*, London 1948

C. F. KELLY and CH'EN Meng-chia, *Chinese Bronzes from the Buckingham Collection, Art Institute of Chicago*, Chicago, 1946

K. Scott LATOURETTE, *A History of Modern China*, London 1954

Berthold LAUFER, *Jade, A study in Chinese Archaeology and Religion*, New York 1912

Sherman E. LEE, *Chinese Landscape Painting*, Cleveland 1954

J. E. LODGE, A. WENLEY and J. A. POPE, *A Descriptive and Illustrative Catalogue of Chinese Bronzes*, Washington 1946

Max LOEHR, *Chinese Bronze Age Weapons*, Ann Arbor 1956

E. McCUNE, *The Arts of Korea*, Rutland 1962

F. MEINERTZHAGEN, *The Art of the Netsuke Carver*, London 1956

F. MEINERTZHAGEN, *Oriental Art*, 1948 onwards

James MICHENER, *The Floating World*, New York 1954

James MICHENER, *Modern Japanese Prints*, Tokyo 1963

H. MINAMOTO, *An Illustrated History of Japanese Art*, Kyoto 1935

T. MITSUOKA, *Ceramic Art of Japan*, Tokyo 1949

MIZUNO Seiichi, *Chinese Stone Sculpture*, Tokyo 1950

MIZUNO Seiichi, *Unkō Sekkutsu: Yün-kang, The Buddhist Cave Temples of the Fifth Century AD in North China* (15 vols, in Japanese with English summary), Kyoto 1952

MIZUNO Seiichi, *Bronzes and Jades of Ancient China* (in Japanese with English summary), Kyoto 1959

Kenji MORIYA, *Die Japanische Malerei*, Wiesbaden 1953

Hugo MUNSTERBERG, *The Arts of Japan*, London 1957

Tochiro NAITO, *The Wall Paintings of Hōryū-ji*, Baltimore 1943

Joseph NEEDHAM, *Science and Civilisation in China*, Cambridge 1951.
The first two volumes of this great work provide a stimulating introduction to the Chinese land, people and ideas.

SEIROKU Noma and TAKESHI Kuno, *Albums of Japanese Sculpture* (6 vols), Tokyo 1953

Robert Treat PAINE and Alexander SOPER, *The Art and Architecture of Japan*, London 1955

John A. POPE, *Fourteenth Century Blue and White: A Group of Chinese Porcelains in the Topkapu Sarayi Müzesi, Istanbul*, Washington 1952

John A. POPE, *Chinese Porcelains from the Ardebil Shrine*, Washington 1956

Alan PRIEST, *Chinese Sculpture in the Metropolitan Museum of Art*, New York 1954

E. O. REISCHAUER and J. K. FAIRBANK, *East Asia: The Great Tradition*, Boston 1960

G. ROWLEY, *Principles of Chinese Painting*, Princeton 1947

R. C. RUDOLPH and WEN YU, *Han Tomb Art of West China*, Berkeley 1951

Alfred SALMONY, *Archaic Chinese Jades from the Edward and Louise B. Sonnenschein Collection*, Chicago 1952

Sir George SANSOM, *Japan: A Short Cultural History*, London 1946

D. SECKEL, *Emakimono*, London 1959

Laurence SICKMAN and Alexander SOPER,

The Art and Architecture of China (Pelican History of Art) London 1956

Osvald SIRÉN, *Chinese Sculpture from the Fifth to the Fourteenth Centuries* (4 vols), London 1925

Osvald SIRÉN, *The Walls and Gates of Peking*, London 1924

Osvald SIRÉN, *The Imperial Palaces of Peking*, Paris and Brussels 1926

Osvald SIRÉN, *The Chinese on the Art of Painting*, Peking 1936

Osvald SIRÉN, *Gardens of China*, New York 1949

Osvald SIRÉN, *Chinese Painting, Leading Masters and Principles* (7 vols), London 1956 and 1958

Basil STEWART, *Subjects portrayed in Japanese Colour Prints*,

E. F. STRANGE, *Japanese Colour Prints*, London 1931

Michael SULLIVAN, *Chinese Art in the Twentieth Century*, London 1959

Michael SULLIVAN, *Introduction to Chinese Art*, London 1961

Michael SULLIVAN, *The Birth of Landscape Painting in China*, London 1962

Peter C. SWANN, *Chinese Painting*, Paris 1958

Peter C. SWANN, *An Introduction to the Arts of Japan*, Oxford 1958

Mai-mai SZE, *The Tao of Painting, a Study of the Ritual Disposition of Chinese Painting* (2 vols), New York 1956

Seiichi TAKI, *Three Essays on Oriental Painting*, London 1920

Kenji TODA, *Japanese Scroll Painting*, Chicago 1935

Staff of the TOKYO NATIONAL MUSEUM, *Pageant of Japanese Art* (6 vols), Tokyo 1952 onwards

I. V. VINCENT, *The Sacred Oasis*, London 1953

Arthur WALEY, *An Introduction to the Study of Chinese Painting*, London 1923, reprinted 1958

Langdon WARNER, *The Enduring Art of Japan*, Harvard 1952

Langdon WARNER, *The Craft of the Japanese Sculptor*, New York 1936

W. WATSON, *Sculpture of Japan*, London 1959

W. WATSON, *China*, London 1961

W. WATSON, *Archaeology in China*, London 1960

W. WATSON, *Ancient Chinese Bronzes*, London 1962

William WILLETTS, *Chinese Art* (2 vols), London 1958

Yukio YASHIRO, *2,000 Years of Japanese Art*, London 1958

Chiang YEE, *The Chinese Eye*, London 1935

Chiang YEE, *Chinese Calligraphy*, London 1954

W. P. YETTS, *The Cull Chinese Bronzes*, London 1939

Lin YUTANG, *Imperial Peking*, London 1961

Index

In brackets after some of the entries in this index the closest convenient pronunciation of some of the Chinese words and names has been inserted. This has only been done where the spelling by which the word or name has always been known in the West leaves the pronunciation in some doubt, and then only where the word or name itself is an important one. These alternative spellings should only be taken as a guide, not as a lesson. They are intended to facilitate familiarity with Chinese words in those readers who are coming across them for the first time and who might be hindered from saying them by uncertainty of their pronunciation.

As a general guide, when ' Ch.. ', ' K.. ', ' P.. ' and ' T.. ' (' Ts.. ' and ' Tz.. ') do not have a ' ' ' after them, they are pronounced as ' J.. ', ' G.. ', ' B.. ', and ' D.. ' (' Ds.. ' and ' Dz.. '): e.g. ' Chin'is pronounced ' jin ', ' Ch'in ' is pronounced ' Chin '. The ' a ' in these words is the Continental ' a ', pronounced like ' u ' as in ' bun '.

Numbers in italics refer to the illustrations on those pages.

Shūbun, painter, *193*, 194
silk, 36, *37*
Silla, state of, 55, 82, 84ff, 130
Sillan period, 97ff, 122, 130, art: 106ff
Sin Yun-bok, painter, 236, *237*
'Six Dynasties', period 61, 68
'Six Old Kilns of Japan', 200
Sōami, painter, 198, *199*
Sokkul-am, cave temple, 107
Sōtatsu, painter, 246
Suchou, 178, 180
Sui dynasty, 97, 99, 105
Sung dynasty, 12 , 135ff, 165, ceramics:
  136, 137ff, *138*, painting: 144ff, *147*,
  tradition: 164, 194, 208

Tai Chin (Dy Jin), painter, 177, 178
Takeuchi Seihō, painter, 263
Tamamushi shrine, 93, *95*
T'ang (Tung) dynasty, 30, 77, 95, 97ff,
  literature: 98, 130, influence: 101,
  102, 105, 107, sculpture: 100ff, paint-
  ing: 108ff, ceramics: 112, *113*, *115*,
  117ff, tradition: 124ff, 141, 150, 175
T'ang yin, painter, 180
Tao Chi (Dao Jee), painter, 231, 232,
  233
Taoism, 33, 35, 82, 98, 150
t'ao-t'ieh, 22
Tempyō period (see Nara)
Tendai, 123
Textiles, 214, *21‹*, 254ff, *256*, techniques:
  256
'The Eight Strange Masters of Kang-
  chou ', 234
' three coloured ' wares, 113
Three Kingdoms period, 84, 85,
  ceramics: 86, 87, 88
ting (ding) wares, *136*, 137, 168, 169
Tōdai-ji temple, 103
Tokugawa Ieyasu, General, 206, 239
Tokugawa period, 198, 207
Tokyo, 240
T'o-pa(Toe-bar) tribe, 64, 84, 95
Tori Triad, 90, 91
Tosa School, 200, 208, 245
Toyotomi Hideyoshi, General, 206, 239
Transitional Period (c. 1620-1650), 185
tsuba, 258
Tun-huang (Dóón-hwarng), cave tem-
  ples, 68, 78, 82, 84, 103, 111
Tung Ch'i-ch'ang (Dóóng Chee-
  charng), 178, 228

T'ung-kou (Tóóng-goe), 84
Turks, 95, 97, 127
Tz'u-chou ware, 154, *155*, 168

ukiyo-e, 240
Unkei, painter, 156
Uragami Gyokudō, painter, 249, 250

Wan-li, Emperor (1575-1616), 185
Wang Chien, painter, 228
Wang Hui, painter, 228, 229
Wang Mêng, painter, 172
Wang Shih-min, painter, 228
Wang Yang-ming, 176
Wang Yüan-ch'i, painter, 228
Wang Wei, painter, 112, 129, 179
Warring States period, 24
Wên Chêng-ming, painter, 178, 179
Wên-jên-hua (Wern-rern-hwa), 179, 202,
  229, 247, 248
Wood work, 93
Writing, 17, 62
Wu (Woo), Emperor (141-86 BC), 47,
  63
Wu Chên, painter, 172
Wu Li, painter, 228
Wu School, 178

Yamato-e, 134, 160, 194, 200, 246, 254
Yang-shao culture, *10*, 11ff.
Yayoi period, 57, 89
Yen Li-pên, painter, 108
Yi dynasty, 192, 202, 235, ceramics:
  202ff, painting: 202
Yi In-man, painter, 236, *237*
Yi Song-gye, General, 202
Ying-ch'ing ware (see *ch'ing-pai*)
Yōsa Buson, painter, 249
Yoshimasa, 192, 194
Yoshimitsu, 192
Yüan dynasty, 165ff, ceramics: *166*,
  167, 168, painting: 171ff, traditions,
  177, 194, 208, 229
Yüeh ware, 44, *45*, 76, *77*, 78, 128
Yün-kang (Yün-garng), cave temples,
  64, *65*, *67*, 82, 140
Yün Shou-p'ing, painter, 228, 229
Yung-lo, Emperor (1403-1424), 185

Zen, 150, 152, 156, 176, 194